ABERDARE

Pictures from the Past

VOLUME TWO

This is a picture by an unknown artist of the Cynon Valley as seen from Fforest farm, Mountain Ash. It was believed by W. W. Price to depict the three meadows said by Malkin to be the 'most engagingly romantic and beautiful' of all views in the Cynon Valley. It is said to date from 1830 and shows what is probably the Aberdare Canal. The buildings to the left of it are hard to identify and they are on the wrong side of the Canal to be Duffryn House

Lord Aberdare

ABERDARE

Pictures from the Past

VOLUME TWO

Published by
CYNON VALLEY HISTORY SOCIETY
1992

ISBN 0 9508586 8 4

Printed in Wales by D. Brown and Sons Ltd., Bridgend, Mid Glamorgan.

INTRODUCTION

The Cynon Valley History Society achieved its 21st anniversary on the 11th March 1992 and this second collection of photographs which is the tenth book to be published by the Society, has been brought out specially to celebrate that event, and to mark with pride many of the Society's other accomplishments.

The first volume of 'Aberdare — Pictures from the Past' published in 1986 proved to be an unqualified success, both commercially and by virtue of the very favourable comments that the book has received from a wide cross section of readers including many in the academic field. A short notice which it received in the prestigious *Welsh History Review* described it as 'A magnificent collection of . . . well captioned photographs vividly illustrating the history of Aberdare which could hardly be bettered.' All 3000 copies of that book have been sold and it has now become both an heirloom and collector's item eagerly sought after in the second-hand book market.

This companion volume closely follows the format of the first in presenting various categories of photographs most of which are here published for the very first time. One of the reasons for the popularity of the first book was the extended captions to the pictures which contain as much information about the picture as can be put into the available space. This practice has been followed in this volume as well. In addition, it is hoped that the usefulness of the book will be increased by the inclusion of an index and cross-references in the captions, both to the previous volume (referred to as 'Vol. 1'), and to *Old Aberdare and Merthyr in Photographs* (referred to as 'OAM') published in 1976 by Stewart Williams.

The photographs have been selected and their historical background researched by a working party consisting of Mr T. J. Evans, Mr J. F. Mear (both of whom participated in the production of the first volume), Mrs Lynne Bryn Jones, who represents the Borough Libraries on the Committee of the Society, and the writer.

If any readers have any old photographs they would like to donate to the Library for posterity or lend to the library for copying (and it should be remembered that old photographs will fade with time and therefore need to be re-photographed before it is too late), they are asked to contact the Librarian or the undersigned. All accessions will be duly acknowledged.

The Society has to thank those who have allowed their photographs to be used for this book and who have helped in other ways. Those photographs not otherwise attributed are from the local history collection of Cynon Valley Borough Libraries, from which the Society has had, as usual, willing assistance. Once again the coloured dust jacket bears the signature 'Mansel'. Based on a photograph dating from about 1905, this painting will appeal to all admirers of Mansel Jones's talents and copies of it (without the lettering) will be on sale in local shops.

Finally the Society expresses sincere thanks to its Publications Officer, Mr John Mear, whose enthusiasm, energy and organization have resulted in the publication of yet another valuable contribution to the history of Aberdare.

Geoffrey Evans
Hon. Secretary
Cynon Valley History Society
December 1992

1   Llyn Fawr occupies a large rock basin or 'cwm' on the northern side of the Craig y Llyn escarpment overlooking the Hirwaun Trading Estate. It was probably formed by the plucking action of a small glacier towards the end of the last ice age. When the ice melted, glacial debris was deposited along the northern edge of the hollow forming a dam behind which a small lake was formed. In 1912 the lake was converted into a reservoir to serve the Rhondda Valley and during this work the famous Llyn Fawr hoard was discovered. This consisted of 24 objects including a sword, sickles, cauldrons, harness fittings and socketed axes. Three of the objects were of iron, the remainder of bronze. The presence of the former led to the dating of the hoard as Early Iron Age *c.*600 BC. It has been suggested that it represents loot probably stolen from a lowland settlement, possibly in the Vale of Glamorgan

2   In the early part of the Bronze Age, Beginning about 1700 BC, the dead were interred in single graves, the body and grave goods being placed in a stone cist or shallow pit, often sealed above by a large capstone, and then, most commonly, covered by a circular mound of local material, stones, earth or turves, forming a 'cairn'. The photograph shows the remains of such a stone cist at the centre of a badly mutilated cairn, situated on a rocky knoll at 389 metres above O.D. on a fairly level spur of the mountain above Cwmbach. The cairn itself must originally have been some 7.6 metres in diameter, built of small stones, whilst the cist would formerly have been 1.3 metres by 0.7 metres and 0.8 metres deep

The Post Office, Hirwaun.

3 The staff of the local post office are lined up for duty in this 1920 view of High Street, Hirwaun, whilst the post master poses in the door-way. The horse drawn vehicle in the centre is probably a parcel waggon. The postal services of Aberdare originally came under Merthyr Tydfil, but by 1852 there were post offices at both Aberdare and Hirwaun. In 1875 the post office at 71 High Street was kept by John Evan George M.R.P.S. who was also a pharmaceutical chemist and druggist and famous for his renowned Pile and Gravel Pills. In 1880 'Letters arrived from all parts (via Aberdare) at a quarter before eight morning and were despatched thereto at a quarter before five afternoon.' The subsequent despatches from Aberdare to all parts of the country were at twenty minutes before six in the evening

4 Much of Hirwaun's industrial history is recalled in this interesting townscape entitled 'A pretty view!' In the foreground is Bute Place, named after the 2nd Marquis who owned the mineral rights and built the houses. Behind Bute Place can be seen (left) Ty Mawr the residence of the various owners of the ironworks which was founded in 1757, and centre the work's blast engine house stack, rolling mill and remains of No.4 furnace. In the background is the bank from which the furnaces were charged, and Crawshay Street (centre) called after William Crawshay who acquired the works in 1819. Right of that is Tudor Avenue (after Tudor Crawshay, Francis Crawshay's son.) in the vicinity of which stood the kilns for calcining the ore. In 1831 900 people worked at Hirwaun, 288 in the iron industry whilst over 600 were employed as colliers and miners

5 Each district of Aberdare had its own 'square', which served as a focal point and where people used to congregate for social purposes. This is a view of Mill Street Square, Trecynon. There are some interesting characters grouped in the photograph including a collier wearing 'yorks'. The business in the background is the Supply Stores ('The Shop for Value') which was owned, *c*.1912–1915 by John Lewis, and noted for its finest quality butter. Trecynon developed rapidly in size and importance after the opening of the Llwydcoed iron-works in 1801 and even held its own cattle fairs in the first half of the nineteenth century. For a view of the other side of the street see plate 15 of OAM

6 This tranquil, almost rural, scene shows the area around the Corner House Inn, Tre-Gibbon, Llwydcoed at the turn of the century. Before the houses were built an ancient highway known as Y Gefyn Ffordd or Heol Adam on the line of the present road marked the boundary of two farms, Pentrebach Farm and Tir Evan Shone Rees. The latter took its name from Ifan ap Shon ap Rhys, a weaver and small holder, the father of the famous radical Unitarian minister and poet Edward Evans, later of Ton Coch, who was born there in 1716. The Corner House and the houses in Tre-Gibbon, which were built to accommodate the workers of the Aberdare Ironworks at Llwydcoed, date from *c*.1801 and were erected by Thomas Jenkin alias Gibbon (probably Thomas ap Jenkin ap Gibbon) of Fforchaman Farm who had acquired Tir Evan Shone Rees by 1800
J.F. Mear

7   This nostalgic scene dating from *c*.1945 recalls the days when children could play in the streets without interference from traffic. The game is probably 'Ring a ring o' Roses' and the location is Mill Street, once the principal street in what is now called Trecynon. In fact the whole area was once called Mill Street (Heolyfelin in Welsh) and it was named after the mill which stood on the east side of the River Cynon. No trace of this can now be seen. In 1853 it was stated 'Mill Street proper is in a very bad state from the ash-heaps of rubbish and filth thrown into and lying on the centre of the road'. 'Ash heaps' are a euphemism for human excreta and other domestic waste which was deposited in the streets. The building at the bottom facing up the hill is the 'Golden Lion' on the tramroad in use from 1848 to 1939

8   Many changes have taken place since this photograph of High Street, seen from its junction with Seymour Street, was taken. The gates on the right of the picture were at the entrance to the burial ground of the parish church. The photograph was taken between 1913 and 1917. During that period the shops opposite the church were occupied by (left to right) J. Chew, Confectioner, J. Chew, Baker, Zachariah and Evans, Undertakers. In 1917 the corner building became Aberdare Urban District Council's public lending library with living accommodation for the librarian, W. Henstone Sturdy. The ivy-covered building is Ty Mawr (see also Pl. 9) which was built in the last quarter of the 18th century. All these buildings were demolished in the 1960s to make way for the Health Centre and its car park

9 Brief reference has been made elsewhere to Ty Mawr (Pl. 8). As previously stated the house was built around 1775 and was then the largest in the village of Aberdare, being referred to in early Parish Registers as 'The Great House'. It was originally the home of members of the Richards family who provided links with Aberdare's agricultural past. In the early 1820s the house became a noted shop and warehouse run by Evan Griffiths, a Carrier who operated boats on the Aberdare and Glamorganshire canals. Ty Mawr later became the home of a number of well known local medical men: Drs Evan Jones, Isaac Banks (his son-in-law) and Harry Banks. Its last owner was Mr Douglas Fowler. The house is seen being demolished in this photograph

10 This early picture of Canon Street shows the magnificent classical facade of one of Aberdare's most important nineteenth century buildings, the Temperance Hall which was erected in 1858 at a cost of £3000 provided by the Total Abstinence Society. The hall, which could accommodate an audience of 1500 also contained a 6 bedroom temperance hotel and a coffee house. In 1895 it became a theatre and in 1918 started showing films. In its temperance hey-day it was the venue of many important public meetings including Henry Richard's great election speech of 1868, and staged numerous spectacular entertainments such as Gilbert and Sullivan's "Mikado", The opera "Blodwen" under Joseph Parry's direction, Minstrel Shows, and appearances by General Tom Thumb

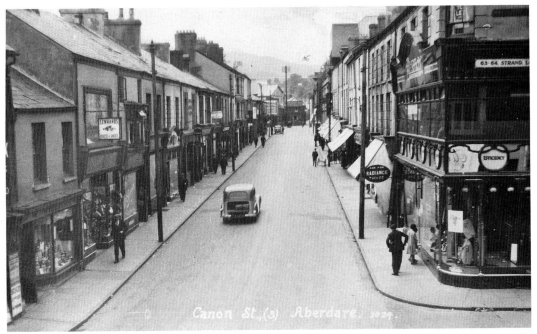

Canon St., (3) Aberdare.

11 This scene recalls the time in the late thirties when there were many fewer motor cars in Aberdare and two-way traffic ran along Canon Street. Prior to 1854 the ground upon which Canon Street and the streets to the north now stand (Maesydre), were open meadows belonging to the Dean and Chapter of Gloucester. In 1800 they were described as being 'so wet and low that they cannot be drained, but as so many horses are kept (there) they are more valuable than they would be otherwise.' Use was however made of these lands during the expansionist period of the mid 1850s and they were parcelled out and let on lease for building purposes in March 1854. The first building to be erected on the Church Estate was the Queen's Hotel which closed in 1923 and is now Burtons. When the Welsh Church was disestablished in 1930 the Freehold ownership of Canon Street and Maesydre passed to the University of Wales

12 A messenger boy carries a parcel on his head whilst a porter or delivery man pulling a hand cart descends Monk Street followed by a bread delivery van, probably belonging to D. Rees Jones of Ynyslwyd Street (see Pl. 38) and a cyclist with a fish frail. The area to the right of this picture was known as Daviestown being built on part of Ynyslwyd farm owned by Griffith Davies whose family is commemorated in such street names as David Price, Griffith, Catherine (seen here), Ann, John, Mary and Elizabeth. The chapel at the bottom of the hill is Carmel, Pen-y-pound first erected in 1812 (enlarged 1832). The colliery to be seen on the mountainside above St. Elvan's is Blaenant Colliery which was sunk by the Aberdare Iron Co.

13 Although referred to as Canon Street in this photograph the focal point of the view is that of the Welsh Harp Square. This square took its name from the public house dating from *c.*1835 which stood on the site now occupied by Woolworth's store. In 1844 the River Dare which now runs under the road was open at this point and had to be crossed by a small wooden bridge known as the Welsh Harp bridge. The square contained one of a number of authorised cabstands located around the town centre. The public house in the centre of the picture is the Central Hotel (originally the Rising Sun). The Fothergill's Arms stands next door but one. To the left of the picture is Lipton's which was opened in 1896. The delivery cart (left) belongs to Ruther, a local fruiterer who had shops in Commercial and Cardiff Streets in 1912

14 (below left) Part of Aberdare's celebrations of Queen Victoria's Jubilee on 22nd June 1897 was intended to be the unveiling of a drinking fountain which Sir William T. Lewis (later Lord Merthyr) presented to the town as a permanent record of the Queen's record reign. Though the fountain was not ready in time a ceremony was held on the spot where it was to be erected. Amongst the dignitaries present were R.J. Rhys (Coroner) and the High Constable (Thomas Lloyd). The Aberdare Volunteers and its band were officered by Col. Thomas Phillips (in uniform). The Council forwarded a congratulatory address to the Queen and each adult pauper in the Parish was given 1/- (5p) and each child 6d (2p). Note how little the buildings in Commercial Place (later Victoria Square) have changed since the taking of this photograph. The people of Aberdare were able to see the actual London Jubilee procession for themselves later that same year on animated pictures shown at the Empire Theatre by means of 'Havard's latest cinematograph'

15 Bad weather cut short this ceremony held on the 10th July 1920 when the statue to commemorate Caradog (Griffith Rhys Jones) and his victories with the South Wales Choral at the Crystal Palace in 1872 and 1873 was unveiled by Lord Aberdare (see Pl. 195 and 196). The bronze statue, the work of William Goscombe John, of Caradog as he was at the age of 40, cost £1500 which had been raised by public subscription. Amongst those present were Caradog's widow (his third wife), his son, Sir William Goscombe John, C.B. Stanton M.P., The High Constable, D.R. Llewellyn and surviving members of the choir some of whom had travelled from China, Canada and the U.S.A.   *J.F. Mear*

16 Commercial Street developed as a shopping centre between 1847 and 1851 and in 1892 was described as 'the leading thoroughfare in the town'. In 1847 it consisted of a rough road flanked by cottages and gardens. By 1851 it had become a busy trading centre which terminated at the old Welsh Harp directly opposite the bridge (see Pl. 17) and contained a variety of shops and public houses, 13 in number by 1880. Its shops in 1852 included a baker, butcher, grocer and tea dealer, tallow-chandler, a watch and clock maker, fishmonger, wood-turner and cabinet-maker. This photograph dates from the 1880s. The barber's pole on the left of the street belongs to John Williams whose Hairdressing and Shaving Saloon for Ladies and Gentlemen boasted American Shaving Chairs, hairbrushing machinery and hot, cold and shower baths!

17 This photograph shows the original iron bridge which spanned the River Cynon linking the area known as the Trap and Abernant with Commercial Street and the town centre. The bridge existed in 1844 as the hotel called after it, and seen on the left (the taller of the two buildings), was known by the name Iron Bridge that year. The gates at the pine end of the Commercial Hotel (right) stand at the entrance of the Glancynon Foundry which was opened by William Williams in 1828. The wording on the gates reads 'Shoeing and general smith work, sawing and wheelwright works'. The bridge seen in the photograph was replaced firstly by another iron-bridge (see Pl. 56 of OAM), and then the present concrete structure. Both the Iron Bridge and Commercial Hotels were demolished to make way for the Aberdare By-pass. The Glancynon Foundry was still operating in the early twentieth century

18 This scene of Cardiff Street, near Victoria Square, certainly suggests the vibrant and busy commercial life of a town which by this time (about 1910) had become quite important. A police-inspector keeps a watchful eye on the town and deliveries of goods are being made. The numerous wooden crates etc., which stand outside the shops awaiting unpacking would have been conveyed there via one of the town's two main railway stations which had extensive goods depots. The building in the centre with flag pole and awning (No. 4 Cardiff Street) was the Aberdare Workmen's Industrial Co-operative Society before the shop was extended and modernised (see Pl. 40). Below that at No. 7, was the Music Stores of Harmston & Co (see Vol. 1 Pl. 160) where in 1892 you could buy a piano for £12.12s (£12.60p) and organs from £5.5s. (£5.25p) or 5/- (25p) per month on the instalment system

19 Many aspects of the social history of Aberdare are captured in this picture, which dates from around the turn of the century, of Cardiff Street. Four horse-drawn vehicles, including a hackney carriage standing at a cabstand are to be seen in the background, whilst a 'horseless carriage' passes along the street. This may be one of the 6 HP. Daimler Wagonettes operated by the Aberdare Valley Motor Service Co. Ltd., which could carry 8 passengers. The building in the left foreground is the National Bank of Wales which since 1932 has housed the local branch of the Midland Bank. Beyond that is the Cardiff Castle Hotel (left with portico and now 'New Look') part of which contained a lively Music Hall in the 1860s whose manager had previously run the Dr. Johnson Music Hall, London

20 This picture of Cardiff Street shows 'The Electric Theatre', a stuccoed temple-like building with twin towers. It was the first of the town's permanent purpose-built picture houses. Also known as the Aberdare Cinema, it opened its doors in 1912 (3 years before William Haggar's Kosy Kinema in Market Street). The 'Electric' gave continuous performances between 2.30 and 10.30 p.m. offering drama, comedy and travel interest films at popular prices ranging from 3d. to 1/- (2½p–5p). When the cinema closed the building was acquired by the Co-op which turned it into a smart food hall long before the days of supermarkets, retaining the balcony for use as a cafeteria. The building later became a D.I.Y. store

21 The person who took this photograph probably intended it to be a view of Windsor Terrace, Abernant, to be seen in the background, and which dates from 1891. In so doing however, the photographer has made an unique and permanent record of Long Row, formerly called Big Row (foreground). These dwellings were amongst the earliest houses at Abernant, having been built for ironworkers prior to 1837. They were double houses, i.e. one above the other, and built along a slope so that access to the upper houses as seen here, was from the top of the slope. A description of Big Row given in a report of 1853 states that 'None (of the houses) have back doors and the lower ones no backlets of any kind. The latter also from their position against a sloping ground are constantly exposed to damp. There are no privies, nor house drains of any kind'
Mrs. Olwen Edwards

22 Lewis Street, Aberaman (part of which is seen here) was the principal commercial centre of Aberaman. This village developed around the ironworks founded by Crawshay Bailey in 1846 and a number of collieries, particularly Aberaman colliery. In 1902 Aberaman had a population of 6000 and was important enough to have its own entry in a Trade Directory whose pages list a number of large shops, a Coffee Tavern, Mineral Water Manufacturer, A Post and Telegraph Office and a variety of shops are to be seen including 'The People's Boot Stores' (right). The large suspended sign (left) in the shape of a watch advertises the location of a clock and watch-maker

23 Tirfounder Road is of unusual width for a street of working class houses. The road is named after Tir-y-ffounder, or 'the land of the founder.' This was originally a homestead owned and occupied by a man who worked at Dyffryn Furnace, a small primitive ironworks, one of three established in the Aberdare area in the late 16th or early 17th centuries by Sussex ironmasters. The Dyffryn Furnace stood on the banks of the Aberpennar brook on the site of the Duffryn or Aberpennar Mill. The houses at Tirfounder would have provided accommodation for miners employed in the adjacent collieries of Lletty Shenkin, Old, Middle and Upper Dyffryn   *J.F. Mear*

Tirfounder Rd. Cwmbach. 1080.

24   The present bus station in Aberdare was once the yard of the G.W.R. low level station. This company had been among the first to introduce bus services to feed their trains, and used the station yard for this purpose. In 1929 their services in south and west Wales were absorbed by a new company, 'The Western Welsh Omnibus Co' though the railway Co retained a 50% interest in it. Here at the Maesydre end of the yard in early Western Welsh days busmen stand in front of the buses which include an A.E.C., a Guy, and also a Thornycroft, one of the G.W.R.'s favourite makes

25   The back of this photograph states that the men are (L. to R., presumably) Tom Jones Williams, Willie Oliver, Trevor Jones all of the George Brewery, and Tom Noot of the Whitcombe Hotel. The car is very interesting, being a Flanders Twenty, made in Detroit, Michigan. As the firm was in business only from 1909 to 1912 we may wonder how one of their cars found its way to Aberdare

26 This is one of the Council's trackless buses, taken at the Depot, probably at the time of delivery around the beginning of 1915, judging by its condition. They were intended as feeders to the trams from the outlying districts (Vol. 1, Pl. 123). The trolley, which ran on the overhead wires, can be seen with its stabilising pendulum. Occasionally the trolley would become detached from the wires, and if this happened on a hill, the trolley would run all the way to the bottom, to the great delight of the children in the streets

27 As early as 1920 the Council tram service began to be augmented by petrol buses starting with seven Tilling Stevens (Vol. 1, Pl. 128). Then, starting in about 1925, the Council started to buy Bristols (above) at a cost of £1,395 each, amassing twelve by 1933. One of these, converted to a tower wagon, survived until the late forties. In those days, the buses had to be suitable for all routes, and so were all single-deckers

28 With the end of the tramway system in sight, the Council began to buy double-decker buses in 1934, starting with an A.E.C., a Daimler, and a Bristol. However, subsequent purchases were Daimlers, (single and double), which came with fluid flywheels and preselector gearboxes. Standing in front of these Daimlers are (L. to R.) ? Jenkins, D.A. Thomas, Alf Lawrence, J. Richards, Albert Airey and Emrys Morgan

29 The Council's last tram ran in 1935, but the buses which superseded them had to make do with the old tram shed at Gadlys (seen here) until the beginning of the sixties. Here the new bus garage is being built (left) and signs of railway activity abound, including a steam engine blowing off in the left background. The Dare Valley branch curves off to the right

30 In the early days of motoring, cars were permitted to go into Aberdare Park, where this photograph was taken. The vehicle has not yet been identified but it probably belonged to the Aberdare Motor Co Ltd. The driver was Francis Waite

31 The Council's Nant Row depot was situated where the car park is at the top of Cross Street and this photograph was taken there. Horse-drawn carts were still in use by the Council, for various purposes, including the collection of domestic refuse, for some years after the war

32 This photograph is of the staff and friends of the 'George' hotel about to start on an outing to Cheltenham in August 1920. The charabanc is a Dennis belonging to the Dare Valley Motor Co. which was formed in 1919. They were later bought out by the G.W.R. whose successor, the Western Welsh Co, continued to use the Dare Valley Co's garage in High St (opposite the telephone exchange) until just before the war. During the war the building was used as a newsprint store

33 This impressive Hirwaun Emporium situated at 41/42 High Street, Hirwaun known as the London Warehouse, was founded by David Davis who was later to become the owner of collieries at Blaengwawr and elsewhere. When David Davis moved to Blaengwawr the business was run by his son Lewis until he became sales agent at Cardiff for his father's coal. The London Warehouse was subsequently acquired by Owen George who traded there as draper, grocer and dealer in sundries. The business was continued by his son, J.O. George and was to become one of Hirwaun's leading establishments

Douglas Williams

34 This shop at 49 Gadlys Road was a drapers for many years. In 1879 the building and No. 51 were occupied by W.Ll. Davies who employed a numerous staff of skilled and experienced hands and 'devoted special care and attention to the mourning department!' It is said that the utmost good order prevailed in all departments. A fascinating glimpse, literally into the window of the past, is provided by this photograph of the shop which had then passed into the ownership of J.M. Evans 'The Cash Draper.' Even this relatively small business had its own dressmaking department on the first floor. Many readers will recognize the rolls of oilcloth to be seen on the left. It has been suggested that the five strange dark sack-like items to the right of the shop front were designed to cover the front of grates during chimney sweeping operation to prevent soot entering the room. The scene dates from *c.*1907   *Elfed Bowen*

35 Although it closed in December 1990, for many years Aberdare's leading and best known Tobacconist's shop was that of A.D. Jones. Its founder Mr Albert Davey Jones, seen at the doorway, was born at the Talbot Inn, Pembroke Street. A.D. Jones entered business and by 1902 was a Cycle Agent in Duke Street. By 1905 he was also selling Gramophones and by 1912 he was dealing in confectionery as well and at some time designed a bike for 5 riders. He eventually became a specialist tobacconist and confectioner trading at 21 Canon Street firstly (above) then at 13b Canon Street. Mr A.D. Jones died in 1959 at the age of 83 but the business continued under the ownership of Mr Trevor Jones, the founder's son. In 1930 the shop offered a large variety of smoking requisites including snuff and 150 brands of Empire tobacco!   *Mr Trevor Jones*

Bank Buildings,

(NEXT DOOR TO LLOYDS BANK)

CANON STREET,

ABERDARE, ... 19..

FROM

PRANCE WILLIAMS,

Specialities:

Millinery, Underclothing

AND BABY LINEN.

Hosiery, Gloves, Umbrellas, Belts, Handkerchiefs and Fancy Neckwear, Etc.

FLOWERS, FEATHERS,
RIBBONS, TULLES,
LACES, SILKS
AND CHIFFONS,
&c., &c.

LADIES' AND CHILDREN'S
COMBINATIONS, CORSETS,
NIGHTDRESSES, CHEMISES,
KNICKERS, CAMISOLES,
VESTS AND BODICES, &c.

ROBES, PELISSES,
FROCKS, COATS,
TUNICS, OVERALLS,
PINAFORES, PETTICOATS,
AND FLANNELS, &c., &c.

36, 37 Most millinery needs could be catered for at Prance Williams judging by the range of items listed on his bill-heading. The business was opened in 1903 and the photograph, showing two of the four assistants employed there, was taken in 1929. The premises which closed in 1931 is now occupied by Halifax Property Services. Mr Prance Williams had a second shop named Paris House (now Halford's) which he opened in 1913 and closed in 1919

Leslie Prance Williams

38   This picture of Halford's and the Cafe Mona was taken *c*.1934. The premises, 2 Commercial Street, were originally occupied by the Welsh Harp stores but by 1867 the building had become the Volunteer Music Hall with its entrance in Dean Street, and later (*c*.1869–1911) the Belle Vue Hotel. Halford's are advertising Meccano, the much coveted children's set of miniature metal parts from which engineering models could be made. The celebrated Cafe Mona of D. Rees Jones & Sons (left of and above Halford's) was partly provisioned by the firm's own farm, Pencoed Dairy Farm, Llwydcoed, and by the bakery in Davies Town. For very many years it was a popular venue for the elite of Aberdare

39   No. 1 Cardiff Street, for many years the premises of William Sarvis, undertaker, silk mercer, linen and woolen draper, milliner and dress-maker (see Pl. 30 of OAM). His business was one of the finest in town and stocked the latest fashions. For example, in 1878 he announced that he 'Begs most respectfully to acquaint his friends and the public generally that he has just returned from London, and on the 15th of May and the following day will be making a striking show of novelles in millinery, bonnets, hats, jackets, mantles, costumes, dress materials and an unusual assortment of fancy goods. An early visit is solicited.' The family and their servants lived above the shop and there was also accommodation for the staff, dressmakers and apprentices who would all have 'lived-in'. William Sarvis retired to The Garth, Hirwaun in 1914 and No. 1 Cardiff Street was subsequently taken over by R.P. Jones & Co., drapers and then by Victor Freed Ltd

40   This photograph dating from *c.*1934 shows the Central Department Store, 'Co-operative House' at 3, 4 and 5 Cardiff Street which housed the society's footwear, grocery and provisions, butchery, men's outfitting, furnishing, electrical and drapery departments. The Aberdare Workmen's Co-operative Industrial Society was established in 1869. At the turn of the century it had 1259 members and paid a dividend of 3/2¼ (16p) in the £. To become a member of the society an entrance fee of 1/- (5p) was required, followed by 3d. (just over 1p) weekly or 3/3d. (16p) per quarter until five £1 shares were paid up. There were various co-operative societies throughout the valley which amalgamated in 1927 to form the Aberdare & District Co-operative Society. Co-operative House closed its doors in May 1988

41   This photograph of the interior of Morris Jacob's shop at 14 Cardiff Street was taken for posterity on the 22nd August 1984 and shows business as it was before the days of self-service and bar pricing codes. Morris Jacob's business was founded in 1874 and closed down only a few years ago. Mr Jacob was a pawnbroker, outfitter and jeweller and advertised the 'cheapest house for new and second-hand clothes' in 1892. Morris Jacob was a Russian Jew and God-father to Mr. Sydney Shimilove who worked in the shop for over 55 years, commencing in 1929 when he was 12 years old and eventually becoming its manager. For many years Mr Shimilove used to travel from Cardiff by bus each day wearing his distinctive brown bowler hat and smart matching 3 piece suit and overcoat

42 Agricultural and seed merchants provided an important service to the community as there were still a number of farms in the area in the first half of this century and more people kept livestock, poultry smallholdings and allotments than do today. This splendid photograph shows the 'Taff Hay and Corn Stores' of William Davies, Hay, Straw, Corn, Seed and Potato Merchant, situated at Duke Street, Aberdare. His advertisements state he was an agent for 'Molassine Meal', and that his terms were 'strictly cash'. The bowler-hatted gentleman holding the scoop is probably the owner Mr. William Davies. The dog would have been 'employed' in keeping down rats. The firm's errand body stands holding his bike

43 Boots and shoes were a staple commodity in an industrial society such as Aberdare and were actually made locally, in places such as Peter Halewood's shoe manufactory in the centre of the town (see Pl. 100 and 181, Vol. 1.) These premises are the Lewis Street, Aberaman branch of J. Mason & Co., Boot and shoe manufacturers whose main business was at Commercial Street, Aberdare. In 1902 this firm solicited made-to-measure orders and repairs and soled men's boots from 2/- (10p) and women's from 1/- (5p). There were 56 boot and shoe makers between Hirwaun and Mountain Ash in 1875

44 This typical ironmongery shop, *c.*1910, was situated in Fforchaman Road, Cwmaman and would have stocked all the hardware requirements of the village. The goods displayed in the window and outside the shop suggest the great variety of items which could be purchased, from brushes to barrels and clothes baskets to children's hoops. As this shop was situated in a mining village the proprietor also sold colliery tools. Many ironmongers were also gasfitters and plumbers

45 On the opposite side of the road from the present day Llwynon Quarry in Penderyn is another large quarry complex consisting of abandoned workings. These were originally separate quarries owned by the various ironworks in Aberdare, the Crawshay Quarry, Gadlys Quarry, Abernant Quarry and Aberaman Quarry. With the demise of the ironworks these ceased working except for the Aberaman Quarry which together with Llwynon Quarry, was acquired by Messrs W.P. Powell, Hirwaun, for the production of roadstone, agricultural limes and flux for the Ebbw Vale Street Works. Both quarries were linked to the G.W.R. at Hirwaun by the Hirwaun Railway. The photograph taken in the early 20th century is of the Aberaman Quarry and shows clearly the characteristic bedding and joining of the limestone. The railway lines run to the quarry face allowing the stone to be loaded directly into the trucks

Richard Evans

46 'The King's Head' was first known of in 1858 when it and the two or three houses to the left of it stood much further back from the road than they do in this picture. By 1919 it was a pub no more but lasted as a dwelling house until after the last war. Its site is a grassy plot and bench at the top of the Gadlys hill, at the entrance to Neville Terrace, which clearly had not been built when this photograph was taken in 1909. A young 'Shoni Winwns' is among the people watching a parade of firemen going down the hill
J.F. Mear

47 The 'Bridgend Inn' stood, predictably, near the end of the Gadlys bridge, which crossed the formation of the railway to Bwllfa. Many a collier on night shift must have had a quick pint in here (and not of Bongola tea) before descending to the platform behind the pub, to take the colliers' train to Bwllfa. The entrance to Pembroke St. (then open to Gadlys Rd.) is on the right. The 'Bridgend' was open by 1872, closed in 1970, and was demolished in August 1973

48   The pub known as the 'Dynevor Arms' once stood on the original Heads of the Valleys road, at its junction with the road which led down the Dyllas to Aberdare. Its site is now part of the roundabout which gives access to Baverstock's Hotel

49   The location of pubs in Abernant has always been peculiar, with two recorded at the bottom end, the Star and Railway and the White Hart, and two at the very top, namely, the Rhos Wenallt (above) and the Halfway house (see Vol. 1 Pl. 15). Opened in 1881, the Rhos Wenallt was an off-licence at first. In September 1888 the landlord applied for a full licence, stating that about 1600 people a week travelled to and fro between the nearby station and Merthyr. The application was granted despite the opposition of the landlord of the Halfway House   *E.J.K. Rees*

Glamorgan County Council,
Technical Instruction Committee.

This is to Certify that Benjamin Davies diligently attended the Phonography Class at Aberdare during the Session of 1894·5 and at the Annual Examination was placed — — in the First Class.

Walter Hogg
Secretary of the Committee.

50 A Parliamentary Act of 1889 gave local authorities powers to provide technical education within their districts. In Glamorgan this was done through the Glamorgan County Council Technical Education Committee. The organising secretary was Walter Hogg, a former headmaster of Park School. Working through a local committee, it provided classes in a number of subjects including Mining, Principles of Agriculture, Mathematics, Applied Mechanics, Welsh, French, Cookery, Geology and many others, as well as Reading, Writing and Arithmetic. The classes were held in local school rooms and students were examined and awarded certificates at the end of each session. The photograph shows a certificate obtained by a successful candidate in phonography (shorthand)   *Nest Evans*

51 Standard V of the Boys Department of the National School in 1908. The National School, the original building of which, dates back to 1829, is the oldest school in Aberdare, although it has now moved to buildings in the grounds of the former Mardy House. This a formal photograph, the scholars being dressed in the their 'Sunday Best' to mark the importance and solemnity of the occasion and they were crowded together to contain them all within the picture. It nevertheless gives a good impression of a classroom layout ninety years ago, with the long, low desks and benches and the large framed pictures on the wall etc. The various objects on the desks were probably intended to convey the impression that a lesson in nature study was in progress

52 The passing of the Forster Education Act of 1870 was a milestone in the history of British education. Local school boards were established to improve the educational needs of the country which had previously been met by British and National (Church) schools. The newly established Aberdare School Board took over several existing British Schools and also built new ones. The first of the latter was in Clifton Street. The School Board continued until 1902 when its responsibilities were handed over to the Aberdare Urban District Council. The Clifton Street school was then known officially as the Town Council School although the old name Board School persisted for many years. After the control of local schools passed to the county council in 1946 it was again renamed Caradog School. The photograph probably dates to the early years of the century

53 Llwydcoed School on St David's Day 1914. It was claimed that this was the first occasion on which an Aberdare School wore traditional Welsh costume. *Back Row*: L.to R. Olwen Edwards, Tegwen Thomas, Maggie May Phillips, Edith Davies, Unknown, Ceinwen Morgan, Violet Cross, Ceinwen Francis, Unknown, Maggie Davies, Edith Griffiths, Mary Francis, Lizzie Cox. *Middle Row*: Unknown, Sarah Davies, Evelyn Davies, Winnie Weston, Daniel Jones, Percy Loader, David Thomas Jones, Annie Evans, Trevor Abbot, Edgar Rowlands, Sam Morgan. *Front Row*: Mr W.W. Price (Headmaster), Unknown, Willie Jones, Mansel Edwards, Lewis James, ? Baker, Will Owen, Unknown, Will Thomas, Joe Owen, Archie Hopkins, Alwyn Evans, Rees Morgan, Miss Annie Evans

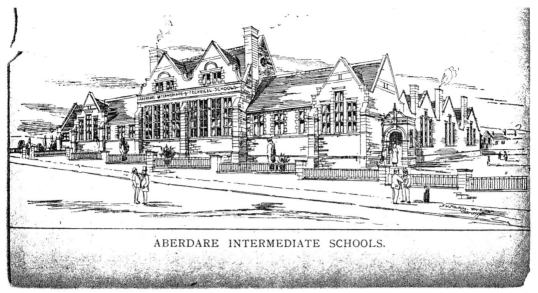

ABERDARE INTERMEDIATE SCHOOLS.

54 As a result of the Welsh Intermediate Education Act of 1889 which authorised the Welsh counties to prepare schemes for the establishment of Intermediate Schools, Aberdare was chosen as the venue for one of the schools in Glamorgan. The selected site was one acre of land opposite the lower entrance to the park, known as 'Commin Bach'. The memorial stone was laid on 10th August 1893 by Lord Aberdare, the president of the committee whose report led to the passing of the Act. The school was officially opened on 28th September 1896 by Mr D.A. Thomas MP. Accommodation was for 100 boys and 80 girls and the catchment area extended from Rhigos to Mountain Ash. The photograph is of the architect's drawing of the school, the main building being substantially that which can be seen at the present day, except for the clock tower which was added some years later

55 In the early 1920s there were some 18 collieries in Aberdare, employing over 10,000 men. The great demand for education and training for the mining industry led to the opening in February 1922 of the Mining Engineering Laboratory attached to the Boys Intermediate School, one of six similar buildings contemplated by the Glamorgan County Council. The photograph shows the official party and guests outside the building. The laboratory was largely due to the initiative of Alderman David Hughes of Aberdare who sadly did not live to see his dream realized. Councillor Mrs Rose Davies (wearing a white scarf in the photograph) formally opened the main door and the ventilating plant and pumping machinery were turned on by County Councillor G.A. Treharne and Dr Robert James of the Treforest School, respectively

56 A 'Keep Fit' class for girls at the Settlement was opened in 1936. It was made possible by the gift of Fairfield House by Mr and Mrs M.H. Llewellyn and by grants from the National Council of Social Service in Wales and from other sources. The prototype of such a settlement was Toynbee Hall in London's East End and the intention was for a group of people to settle in a deprived area to study and to make provision for the needs of the community. In the mid 1930s there were 6000 people out of work in Aberdare and it was estimated that 1 person in 3 was unemployed or was a dependant of one. The Settlement was officially opened by Dr W.G. Adams, Warden of All Saints and the first warden was Mr J. Victor Evans, M.A., Barrister at Law, supported by ten specialist staff

57 A men's carpentry class at a Social Centre. The activities available were many and varied. The cultural activities at the settlement itself included English Literature, Economics Theory, Welsh, French, International Politics and Current Affairs. At that time there were throughout the valley a number of social service centres and it was through these that the settlement was able to keep in touch with the unemployed and their families. Here music and drama groups were set up and a variety of practical activities provided, such as needlework and quilting for women and interior decorating, carpentry and bootmaking and repairing for men. There was great emphasis on physical fitness with 'Keep Fit' clubs for men, women, girls and boys. Some cultural activities were also extended to the outlying centres

58 Although there were early 19th century precedents it was not until the Boer War that there was a serious attempt to raise a yeomanry unit in Glamorgan. This was the Glamorgan Company of the Imperial Yeomanry which eventually in 1908 became the Glamorgan Yeomanry – a unit of the newly designated Territorial Army. Because they were usually required to provide their own horses and saddlery, the Yeomen were normally young farmers or came from the better off sectors of the community. Individual troops such as the Aberdare Troop were formed on a territorial basis. It is shown here at the first annual camp of the newly formed regiment at Margam Park in 1908   *Elfed Bowen*

59 Three stalwart local gentleman who volunteered for service during the Great War. They were over the age limit for active service but nevertheless undertook a part-time engagement involving home duties. Based at the Drill Hall on Cwmbach Road, they performed local guard duties, but their main function was to act in support of the police force if and when necessary. From left to right they are – Mr Tom Evans who kept a grocery shop in Maesydre; Mr John Young, a relieving officer; Mr Saunders Morgan, a well known local tailor. Mr Young had previously served with the local Volunteer Corps
Mrs Haulwen Marsh

60 Germany's invasion of Belgians in 1914, the nominal reason for Britain's entry into the war, evoked a tremendous feeling of outrage throughout the country. About a million Belgian refugees fled their country and by the end of 1914, nearly 200,000 had arrived in Britain. Aberdare received its quota and several families were accommodated in the recently built New Scales houses in Llwydcoed and in the Stag Hotel, Trecynon. The photograph shows a group of refugees outside New Scales Houses which decades later were still referred to as the 'Belgian Houses'

61 The photograph taken outside the Boot Hotel in the early months of the Great War is of an ambulance provided by the local branches of the Royal Antediluvian Order of Buffaloes together with a team of Voluntary Aid Detachment (V.A.D.) nursing members. It seems as though this was some kind of an official occasion as a number of the men present are wearing ceremonial chains, most of which indicate holders of office in the R.A.O.B. The ambulance and nurses were intended to deal with the reception of wounded soldiers who were accommodated in the Trap Surgery before the opening of the General Hospital. The lady in nurse's uniform 5th from the right is Miss Mabel Saunders Morgan who later was to become the wife of Mr David Davies (see Pl. 67)   *Mrs Haulwen Marsh*

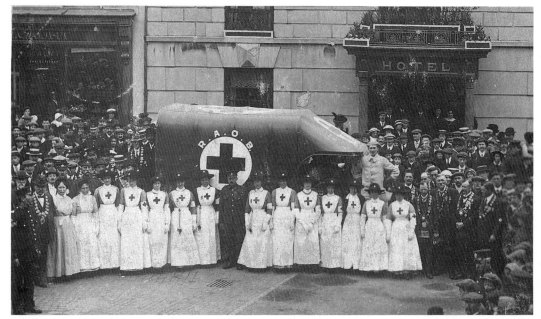

62 During the Great War, churches and chapels were still very strong and each maintained very close links with those of its members in the armed forces. Every service man on his departure was given a small pocket New Testament. The photograph shows Bethel Women's Society for Soldiers' Parcels with the minister's wife Mrs Jacob seated in the armchair in the centre. Bethel drew its members virtually from within a radius of a quarter of a mile from the chapel. Yet from this small area 14 of its congregation died. Their names were commemorated on a memorial plaque which has now been removed to Ebenezer Chapel *Elfed Bowen*

63 Nearly ¾ million men from the U.K. were killed in the Great War. According to the British practice they were buried in military cemeteries in France, Belgium and other theatres of war. Relatives wishing to pay their own tribute and perpetuate the memory of their loved ones, frequently had memorial cards produced giving personal details and often a photograph of the dead serviceman. The 13th Battalion was a Service Battalion (raised for the duration) of the Welsh Regiment and was initially recruited in 1914 chiefly from the Rhondda and Cynon Valleys. The traditional spelling of Welch with a 'c' was suspended during the war and was not resumed until 1920 *Mrs Dilys Evans*

IN LOVING MEMORY

OF

Private WILLIAM ARTHUR STEPHENS

(13TH BATTALION WELSH REGIMENT),

*Dearly beloved Son of E. and M. Stephens,
69, Jubilee Road, Godreaman, Aberdare,*

Who was Killed in Action on October 8th, 1918,

near Cambrai,

And was Buried at Malincourt, a few miles away from the
town of Villers Outreaux.

AGE 19 YEARS.

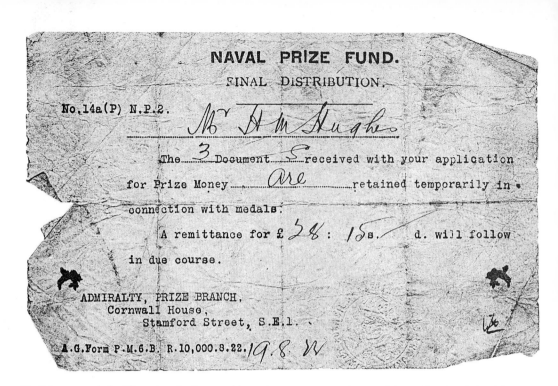

NAVAL PRIZE FUND.

FINAL DISTRIBUTION.

No.14a(P) N.P.2. *Mr H M Hughes*

The *3* Document *s* received with your application

for Prize Money *Are* retained temporarily in

connection with medals.

A remittance for £ *28* : *15* s. d. will follow

in due course.

ADMIRALTY, PRIZE BRANCH,
   Cornwall House,
     Stamford Street, S.E.1.

A.G.Form P.M.6.B. R.10,000.8.22. *19.8 W*

64 Prize money derived from the sale of enemy ships and property captured at sea. Prior to 1914 the whole of the money went to the ship's company that did the capturing. After that date all prize money was pooled and shared out throughout the Navy as a whole, the actual amount received depending on the rank of the recipient. Mr Hughes who served on destroyers during the war, subsequently became Works Superintendent of the Transport Department of the Aberdare Urban District Council

Mrs Dilys Evans

65 Aberdare Peace Celebration November 1918. After the Armistice on the 11th November 1918, Aberdare in common with other towns throughout the United Kingdom celebrated with scenes of wild patriotic rejoicing. C.B. (John Bull) Stanton, a former socialist who had been elected as the local M.P. following the death of Keir Hardie in 1915 is in the centre of the photograph. Stanton's pro-war stance earned him the soubriquet 'the man who beat the Germans at home'. However it should be remembered that his only son Clifford, was killed in the Third Battle of Ypres in 1917. In December 1918, shortly after this photograph was taken, in the notorious 'Coupon Election', Stanton was again elected, securing a convincing victory over his I.L.P. opponent, the Rev. T.E. Nicholas

66 Aberdare Cenotaph was unveiled on the afternoon of Thursday, 8th March 1923. Over 20,000 people attended the ceremony, to pay tribute to the 700 Aberdare men who fell in the Great War. After the singing of 'Our God our help in ages past' and a reading by the Rev D. Silyn Evans, Sir D.R. Llewellyn removed the Union Jack which hung on the memorial. The 'Last Post' was sounded and the dedication of the Cenotaph by the Vicar of Aberdare took place. There followed 'Reveille' and the national anthem. Wreaths were then laid. Scout Charles Henry Wiltshire whose father had been killed in the war placed one in the centre of the Cenotaph on behalf of local ex-service men. The photograph taken after the ceremony shows Scout Wiltshire in the foreground and many of the dignitaries present including (in front of the Cenotaph) Sir D.R. and Lady Llewellyn, Mr Illtyd Williams (High Constable) and Mrs Williams and the Vicar, the Rev. J.A. Lewis

67 The two special constables in this World War II photograph are Mr Ernest Evans, coal merchant on the right and Mr David Davies, provision merchant. Mr Davies is well known to all Aberdarians. He served with the Welsh Regiment during the Great War as a sergeant Lewis gunner and was wounded twice. He fought in the Battles of the Somme and Third Ypres and in the latter participated in the successful attack on Pilkem Ridge. Mr Davies has played an active part in the religious and cultural life of Aberdare. He is still an avid reader particularly of historical works and is a keen and critical follower of sport especially of rugby football. Recently he celebrated his 106th birthday making him the oldest surviving member of the Welsh Regiment (now incorporated into the Royal Regiment of Wales) and probably the oldest man in the principality

Mrs Haulwen Marsh

68 Civil Defence groups formed during the Second World War included besides the police and fire services, air raid wardens, firewatchers and communications personnel. They were trained to deal with incendiary bombs, gas attacks and were intended to provide an organization to deal with the worst scenario of all, the aftermath of a big air raid. The photograph is of some Aberdare Town Civil Defence Officers. Back Row (L. to R.) John Lewis (Hairdresser), David Emrys Evans (Chemist), J.T. Bowen (Grammar schoolmaster), ? Evans (Cooperative Works Department). Front Row (L–R) Ernie Reynolds (Surveyor), Miss Wyke (Maindy Place), P.C. Frank Ballinger; Mrs Olga Lloyd, Noel Thomas (Chemist)

69 The Hirwaun Industrial Estate was originally built in 1942 as a Royal Ordnance Factory for the purpose of manufacturing munitions. It was acquired by the Board of Trade in 1945. Many of the buildings were then converted to accommodate peacetime factories, others were demolished and rebuilt. The Dalek-like structure shown in the photograph stands outside the office block on the estate. It is a steel air raid warden's shelter which stood on the roof of a building since demolished which occupied the same site. The inscription on it, on which these notes are based, points out that it is the sole surviving relic of the wartime role of the estate

70 When the Vale of Neath line was opened on 23rd September 1851 its terminus was at Aberdare on a branch line, not at the intended destination, Merthyr, the line to which was not ready. Passengers from Neath wishing to go to Merthyr got off at a temporary station called 'Merthyr Road' and finished the journey by horse-drawn vehicles. An anecdote in a Chapel history led to the discovery a few years ago of the location of this station (above) which was converted to a house when no longer required. It stands a little distance from the Hirwaun to Merthyr road where it crosses the line   *J.F. Mear*

71 Llwydcoed station on the Merthyr branch in July 1962, a photo taken from the road bridge with a train for Merthyr. The train was perhaps running late, as the guard appears to be a little impatient as he watches the few passengers alight. British Railways had already announced that the line was to close, and this took place on the last day of December that year

72 On the 1st of February 1865 the Vale of Neath Railway was taken over by the Great Western Railway and the line to Aberdare was eventually extended via Pontypool Road to the Midlands and the North, becoming an important route. On the 13th of June 1964 passenger traffic ceased and all that now remains of the original line in this area is the portion from Rhigos estate to Cwmbach, where the line now diverges to join the 'low level' line. Here the guard waves away the last train from Aberdare to Pontypool Road

73 Immediately after its closure to passenger traffic in June 1964, the double track through Aberdare high level station (the present station) was 'singled', as this photograph shows. Motor parcel vans are still in evidence outside the goods shed, which was the original passenger station dating from the opening of the line. In later years this building, by then a rarity, was sadly destroyed by fire. In 1988 the station was further altered to permit the resumption of passenger trains

74 In 1932 the G.W.R. agreed to run a Sunday school excursion train from Cwmaman to Porthcawl, but for safety reasons they refused to run the laden train over the Cwm and Gamlyn viaducts, insisting that everyone got off at Black Lion halt (Monk St) and walked down to the high level station to rejoin the train! Eventually they relented and the trip (above) took place on 23rd July, 1932, the train running in two parts. Similar excursions took place in 1933, 1934, and 1935

75 This photograph dates from about 1910 and is of Aberaman station, originally called Treaman, looking towards Aberdare. It was sited in front of Glancynon Terrace and the Aberdare bypass now runs along this route. The line joining from the left was a private line from Cwmaman belonging to the Powell Duffryn Co., while the line turning off to the left at the end of the platforms is the siding for the Abergwawr Colliery, traces of which can still be seen alongside the bypass at the Aberdare end of Glancynon Tce

76 The almost complete lack of weather protection for the footplatemen of this engine is typical of a middle-period G.W.R. engine, though cabs were fitted retrospectively in later years. The photograph was taken outside the old shed at Aberdare, the rear wall of which can still be seen abutting the Tramway. The shed was built in 1867 and doubled in size in 1874. The engine was built in 1870 and belongs to the 1016 class, another of which, no. 1072, blew up with the loss of two lives at Gooseberry Hill on the Cwmaman branch in May 1874. The boiler left the frames and landed '200 yards away at least' in a field where it was left for nearly 30 years

77 In the first decade of the century many railway companies became aware of the advantages of 'rail motors' (a steam-powered single carriage). The G.W.R. ran them on suburban and valley branch services (Vol. 1, Pl. 112) as did the T.V.R., which owned 19 at one time, of which the above is one. They were used on the shuttle service between Mill St Platform (at the bottom of Meirion St) and Commercial St Platform (near the Rugby Club) which started in 1904. This service was later extended to the low level station and afterwards to Pontypridd. They were also used on the colliers' service to Nantmelin

78 A view of Aberdare engine shed, from the 'open' end (compare Vol. 1, Pl. 105) taken in 1962, 3 years before closure. The locomotive is no. 5237, a design by Churchward, built in 1910 for heavy freight work   *T.J. McCarthy*

79 Although not very conveniently situated for the village, Hirwaun station on the Pontypool to Neath line was busy enough as the number of staff in this photograph shows. Commercial traffic came from the adjacent brickworks and the Penderyn quarries 2 miles away, while during and after the war goods and passenger traffic came from the Rhigos estate. This postcard was sent in 1909 by a Hirwaun girl to tell her aunt in Gamblyn Tce that she had arrived home safely after visiting her!   *J.F. Mear*

Hirwain Station.

80 Hirwaun station was the junction for Merthyr, the line passing through Llwydcoed and Abernant before tunnelling through the mountain at Blaen-nant-y-groes (seen after closure in 1962). As this line was originally intended to be the main line the tunnel was made wide enough for two broad-gauge tracks, though traffic never made the doubling necessary. This branch was difficult to build and bankrupted two contractors during the 6 years of its construction   *Hans Hoyer*

81 Also by Hans Hoyer is this fine shot of the platform at Aberdare (Low Level) with a Diesel Multiple Unit waiting to start for Cardiff. Compare the view of the earlier building (taken from the opposite direction) at Pl. 103 of Vol. 1

82 Everything seen in this photograph dating from the early 1960s has disappeared and has been replaced by the roundabout and bypass. A Morris ambulance waits as a train of small coal runs through the much-hated Commercial St level crossing on the low level line. The photograph was taken from the footbridge referred to in another view of this crossing in Vol. 1, Pl. 8

83 The ironstone deposits which supplied the local ironworks frequently occurred at shallow depths beneath the surface, hence the usual method of working was by a kind of quarrying known as 'patching'. The waste material from the workings was deposited in long, low, fan-shaped tips, the spoil being carried thence over temporary tramways which were extended as the tips advanced. These derelict tips, quite distinct from the coal spoil tips now being reclaimed, are a familiar feature of the 19th century industrial landscape of N.E. Glamorgan and are well exemplified in this photograph of Fothergill's Patches about a mile N.W. of Llwydcoed village   *Tom Evans*

84 Molten iron from the blast furnaces was led into a sand bed in which there were several main channels (sows), from which shorter channels (pigs) led off at right angles. In the latter the metal cooled and solidified, hence the term 'pig iron'. The whole arrangement was known as a pig bed and sometimes as in this case it was enclosed by a cast house. The building fronts the furnace bank of the former Gadlys ironworks which contains the remains of four blast furnaces. The bricked-up archways are the original entrances. It dates from the mid 1850s when the reconstruction of the Gadlys works was completed. Until recently it was used as a council main store, but is now derelict. In 1989 it was classified as a Grade II Listed Building   *Tom Evans*

85 These buildings known as Office Houses were the offices of the Abernant Ironworks. They were probably built in the 1820s as part of the expansion of the works following its acquisition by the Aberdare Iron Company and were originally known as Abernant Place. The trees in the background covering the spoil tip were planted in the 1850s by Richard Fothergill III (Pl. 109) to screen his residence, Abernant House (now Aberdare Hospital) from the ironworks. Access to the summit of the tip was obtained by flights of steps on either side, some of which remain today and are known to the older residents of Abernant as the 'Hundred Steps'   *Tom Evans*

86 William Crawshay II acquired the Hirwaun Ironworks in 1819 and completely refurbished them. From the outset the works were only intermittently successful and their mixed fortune continued even after Crawshay's eldest son Francis (see Pl. 106) took over management in 1841. Francis bought Hirwaun from his father in 1855, but continued deterioration resulted in the complete closure of the works in 1859 and two years later it reverted to the landlord, the Marquis of Bute. The stone block shown in the photograph taken in 1942, was found lying by the side of the Glamorganshire Canal in Cardiff. It measured 7′ × 3′ × 2′ and was probably incorporated into part of the fabric of the works to indicate Francis Crawshay's ownership. Apparently it was conveyed to Cardiff in a truck, but the reason for its removal from Hirwaun remains a mystery
J.F. Mear

87 The Aberdare Canal was opened in 1812 and feeder tram roads were built as indicated in Pl. 88. The canal company acquired what amounted to running powers over the Llwydcoed-Hirwaun section of the earlier Tappendens' tramroad almost immediately (Pl. 89), and in 1841 they obtained complete control of it. The limits of canal companies' properties were defined by iron or stone boundary markers. The one shown is that of the Aberdare Canal Company (ACN–Aberdare Canal Navigation), near the eastern end of the stone tram road bridge at Gelli Isaf. It was probably put there after their purchase of the tramroad land in 1841
Glyn Davies

88 The old tram road bridge at Robertstown was included in the first volume of pictures from the past (Pl. 78). This photograph shows one of the upright bars on the deck of the bridge, which carries the legend ABERNANT 1811, i.e. the maker's name – Abernant Ironworks and the date of erection. The bridge carried the Aberdare Canal Company's tramroad from Canal Head to its connection with the Tappendens' tramroad (see Pl. 89) at Gelli Isaf. In 1827 a link was made with the Gadlys Ironworks at its western end. One of the oldest surviving iron railway bridges in the world, it was restored some years ago and has been scheduled as an Ancient Monument   *Glyn Davies*

89 The terminus of the Neath Canal shown here was linked to Aberdare's early industrial development. In 1805, the Tappendens, partners in the Abernant Ironworks, built a tram road from their works, through the Llwydcoed works, through Hirwaun, connecting with the ironworks there, thence over Cefn Rhigos and down Cwm Gwrelych by means of an inclined plane to the canal basin at Abernant (Glyn Neath). Iron from all three works was sent over this tram road and exported via the Neath Canal until about 1814, after which only Abernant's trade continued and that only for a few years. This was due to the opening of the Aberdare Canal. Traffic virtually ceased on the Neath Canal in 1921, so judging by the number of barges seen, the photograph was probably taken in the early years of this century   *Tom Evans*

90 An old level at Cwmdu Uchaf near Robertstown, of which virtually nothing is known. The drystone lining of this level must have been a tedious and backbreaking task. Now nature is re-asserting herself and the walls are bulging and in a dangerous condition. The tree roots breaking through the roof show that this view was taken just inside the entrance. Collapses occurring just inside are very dangerous because the overburden is not thick enough to support itself and usually falls in and blocks the level up. Keep out! *Steve Grudgings*

91 Although it closed in 1939 the Gadlys pit was kept in working order for maintenance purposes until the early 1970s when it was demolished (above). Attempts by the National Museum of Wales, the District Council and the History Society to preserve the pit nearest the town centre had failed. Although called the 'New pit' (as well as the 'Victoria pit') it dated from 1844. Wherever there is a New pit there is an Old pit, which in this case stood where the eastern end of Lambert Tce now is. The winder and headframe shown here are obviously not original (compare Vol. 1, Pl. 60)

92 In the heyday of the coal industry taking visitors underground was a common occurrence. Here are some visitors about to be conducted down Powell's Pit in Cwmdare (Bwllfa No 3) by the General Manager, W.M. Llewellyn (left). They are standing outside the smith's shop and the winding engine house is seen in the background

93 When opencast coal mining is taking place it is not unusual for the contractors to break into old workings. In the summer of 1992, at the opencast site to the north of Moss Row, Abernant, two old drams were found in such works, of which this is one, still filled with coal. The contractors, Messrs Walters, kindly presented the drams to the Dare Valley Country Park where they are now kept. They probably date from the first quarter of the century   *J.F. Mear*

94 At the bottom of Tudor Tce and next to the footbridge to Robertstown (since altered) there was once a level from which water used to run known as the Horseway level or Aberdare level. From an old mining map it appears to run into the six foot workings of the Park Pit, which was at the end of Broncynon Tce, Cwmdare. Here it is being connected to concrete pipes about ten years ago before being covered over *Douglas Williams*

95 Although thought to be in the Cynon valley, the location of this scene has not yet been ascertained. It was probably taken outside a small level from which a haulier is about to leave with a load of house coal. Two well-laden drams are seen in the background *Douglas Williams*

96 One of the collier's skills was that of 'racing' a dram, that is, of loading it as shown to carry as much coal as possible. The skill lies in building up the coal in such a way that none of it would fall off during its progress from the face to the top of the pit. For payment purposes, the collier's number is chalked on the side of the dram, which is prevented from moving by a wooden 'sprag' thrust between the spokes of a wheel   *National Museum of Wales*

97 In this view of the fan engine house at Bwllfa Colliery in about 1910 there is a two cylinder steam engine driving the fan by multiple rope drive, which is typical of the time. However, the engine is designed to work one cylinder at a time so that the other can be repaired or maintained. Therefore the connecting rod and eccentric rods of the nearer cylinder are disconnected and 'triced up' to the roof beams with chains. The man on the right stands at the wheel of the steam admission valve but the wheel for the other cylinder (right foreground) has been removed. Through the arch can be seen another fan drive   *National Museum of Wales*

98 The development of the coal industry in the valley of the river Aman started at its threshold at Aberaman, where Crawshay Bailey sank a pit in 1845 and built an ironworks (Vol. 1, Pl. 49 and 58). Other pits followed, including this one, Fforchaman, or Brown's pit, which was begun in 1852 by seven businessmen from Gwent. The colliery closed in 1965/66 and the area has been landscaped. Note the Maclean tip in the background

99 Here is another view of Fforchaman Colliery with some Aberdare Rotary Club members about to descend the pit accompanied by officials. From left to right they are: T. Baker, V. Freed, A. Freed, A.B. Andrews, G. Trevor Jones, Ernest King (Rotary Secretary), J.A. Price (Agent, Powell Duffryn), M. Gulliver (Under Manager), W.J. Hodges (President), Ben Roderick, J.L. Rowlands, G.T. Harvey, Edgar Hodges, Gwyn Bevan and Mr Walter Jones (Manager)

100 Other pits in the Aman valley were the Cwmneol, Bedwlwyn, Fforchneol, Trewen, Cwmaman and Fforchwen (above). The last two named were the main centres of production and were known locally as Old and New Shepherd's pits respectively. Though sinking started at Fforchwen in 1874 it was not brought to completion until 1897. This picture taken in about 1920 shows the cooling pond (bottom left) with the power house behind. Like most of the pits in the valleys, it only worked intermittently during the 1920s. It closed finally in 1934

101 Cwmneol Colliery was developed in 1847–1851 and was also known as Morris's pit after one of its promoters. The men in this picture are officials of the pit who continued working during the 'Cambrian strike', being escorted to and from work. The Cambrian strike started in the autumn of 1910 with a dispute at the Naval Colliery, Penygraig, over the price for cutting the upper five foot seam, and by the beginning of November there were 30,000 men on strike in the coalfield and much violence, including the famous 'Tonypandy riots'. The strike ended inconclusively in August 1911   *Douglas Williams*

102   Acquired in 1914 from its previous owners by the well-known D.R. Llewellyn, Dyllas Colliery stood about a third of a mile to the north-east of Grey's Place in Llwydcoed, but received its electrical power from Llewellyn's power house at the Gadlys (still standing), which was driven by the exhaust steam from the nearby Council power station. The output from this colliery was taken down an incline to the Hirwaun-Merthyr railway line where, a couple of hundred yards to the east of Moriah place, the ruins of the above tipping plant and sidings can still be seen

103   Writing in 1815, Walter Davies wrote 'The hill between Aber Dar and Merthyr Tudful is perforated with levels'. The main purpose of these levels, and the pits which followed from about 1840, was to provide coal for the ironworks. Such a pit was the Abernant No 9 pit, seen here and in Vol. 1, Pl. 53, though its location was in fact nearer Cwmbach than Abernant, being 200 yards or so north of Ynyscynon House. Connected originally to Abernant ironworks by the Abernant railway, it was connected to the Taff Vale Railway in later years. It closed in 1910

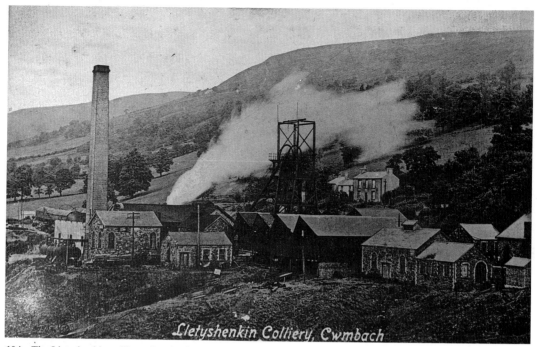

Lletyshenkin Colliery, Cwmbach

104 The Lletyshenkin colliery, Cwmbach, was started in 1843 by William Thomas, son of Lucy Thomas, the so-called 'Mother of the Welsh steam coal trade'. The first coal was sent out in March 1845. By 1896 it was in the possession of Burnyeat, Brown and Co. It was a dangerous pit, and as early as 1849 an explosion claimed 53 lives, a death toll exceeded in this valley only by the Middle Duffryn explosion of 1852, when 68 died. Among the 53 were 13 boys aged from 8 to 15 and there were 5 instances of a father and two sons being killed. Other explosions there in 1853 and 1862 cost 4 lives each. It closed in 1922, not much lamented

105 In the 1960s this dramatic accident happened near the Tower Colliery. An engine and some loaded wagons were coming down from the associated Tirherbert colliery and stopped at the top of a gradient for the brakes of the wagons to be applied by hand. However, before this could be done the wagons ran away, pushing the engine before them. The result was that the runaways collided with the screens which collapsed upon them, tearing away from the overland conveyor (upper right), which has been provided with an emergency support made of a 'cog' of sleepers

Douglas Williams

106 Francis Crawshay was one of the sons of William Crawshay the second, and he was put in charge of the firm's works at Treforest, where the pig iron from Hirwaun was refined. Afterwards he took charge of Hirwaun as well but refused to live in the manager's house, preferring to build a cottage for himself. He was very popular, partly because he could speak Welsh but also because of his humour, kindness and eccentricity. He retired to Sevenoaks, where, until prevented by his neighbours, he would walk around his grounds dressed in nautical dress, striking huge bells that hung here and there   *Douglas Williams*

108 David Davis 'Maesyffynon' must be distinguished from his father, David Davis 'Blaengwawr', who started as a grocer at Hirwaun (see Pl. 33) and became a successful speculator in coal mining in the mid 19th century. The son was more of a public figure than his father, being interested in education, politics, and religious matters. He was a good employer and kept his collieries open during the 'lock-out' of 1875, and later became vice-chairman of the Conciliation Board

107 Lewis Noah Williams entered into partnership with Evan Thomas of the Cambrian Lampworks (see Pl. 111) and eventually became its sole proprietor. He lived adjacent to the works in the house called Caecoed. He was the son of the illustrious William Williams ('Y Carw Coch') who built the Stag inn in Trecynon and founded a series of Eisteddfods there. The son published a collection of his father's poetry in 1908

109 The Fothergill family was one of the several which came down from the north of England and became successful in the iron and coal businesses. This is Richard Fothergill III who was placed in charge of the Aberdare (i.e. Llwydcoed) and Abernant iron works in 1846 by the then owner, his uncle Rowland Fothergill, Richard subsequently became the first M.P. for Aberdare and Merthyr. A descendant of his, John Fothergill, who was also a grandson of Francis Crawshay, became well known after publishing his experiences as an innkeeper before and during the war

110 Although the foundation stone of the Cynon Tinplate Works was laid in 1850 by Thomas Wayne who intended it as an adjunct to the Gadlys Ironworks, it was not actually built until 1868. Production began the same year under Messrs Chivers, Smith & Co and about 150 people were employed. There followed a succession of owners until in 1890 the plant was acquired by Richard Thomas & Co when there were 4 mills in use. The photograph taken in the 1880s by J. Lendon Berry shows a group of tinplate workers outside the works which was situated on the west side of the Vale of Neath line, immediately south of the Robertstown crossing. The tongs held by several of the men were for handling the hot sheets of iron (later steel) when they were passed through the rolls and when they were dipped into the baths of molten tin. Note also the protective leather aprons. The works closed in 1928 and were dismantled in 1941

111 The Cambrian Lampworks is Aberdare's oldest surviving manufacturing concern. It started in 1860 when Mr Evan Thomas opened an ironmonger's shop in Cardiff Street and began making safety lamps. He was soon joined by Mr L.N. Williams (see Pl. 107) and the business rapidly expanded since the burgeoning South Wales coal industry provided a ready market. The firm now moved to new premises in Graig Street (shown in the photograph). In 1884, a Royal Commission on Mines instigated a series of tests on safety lamps from Britain and the continent and it was adjudged that the Evan Thomas No. 7 gave the best results. Subsequently the Company won many other prestigious awards. There is a continuing demand for safety lamps for gas testing and Cambrian Lamps still has a worldwide market. The Graig Street building was destroyed by fire in January 1978 after which the firm moved to new premises on the Robertstown Industrial Estate *Tom Evans*

112   In 1902 a small brickworks, trading under the name of the Tanybryn Brickworks Company, was established on the site of the former ironworks at Llwydcoed (see OAM, Pl. 55). The raw material was the shale from the adjacent spoil tips of the old ironstone workings, which was particularly suitable because of its low carbonaceous content. The bricks were fired in beehive kilns. Although the work was arduous, there was traditionally a high proportion of female labour as indicated in the photograph of the work force assembled in front of the kilns. A new brickworks was set up on the same site by D.R. Llewellyn in 1913 and this, under various owners and with several modifications persisted until 1981   *J.F. Mear*

113   The Powell Duffryn Pipeworks at Aberaman specialised in the production of salt-glazed earthen sanitary pipes and various accessories. The basic raw material was clay, originally obtained from a level in a field behind the works. This was puddled into a stiff plastic mass which was then fed into machines which by a die-casting process produced semi-plastic pipes and fittings. These were transferred to the drying shed and then to the beehive kilns for firing, during which the salt glazing took place. The source of heat for the drying shed was steam from the colliery and coal was used in the kilns. With the closure of the Aberaman Colliery in 1962, gas was substituted in each case. The plant finally closed in 1967. The photograph taken probably in the late 1950s shows stock piles of finished pipes, with beehive kilns and the drying shed in the background   *Hans Hoyer*

114   The photograph taken in 1905 shows the workshops of Vicary and Co in Dean Street. The firm, originally Vicary and Lanman was founded in 1880, but the partnership was dissolved about 1900 and Charles Reuben Vicary carried on his own coach building business in Aberdare. The two storey premises in the picture included a smithy and workshops with facilities for body makers, wheelwrights, painters and other craftsmen. All types of vehicles were made, ranging from light carriages to wagons and railway vans and later ash-carts, delivery vans and even fire engines. Soon after he started, William Morris wrote to Mr Vicary asking him to take on the first Morris car agency in Wales. Mr Vicary rejected the offer. The works finally closed in 1930
Charles Vicary

115   When the Aberaman Ironworks and Colliery were purchased by the Powell Duffryn Company in 1866, iron making was carried on briefly, but within a few years the ironworks site was converted to an engineering works. The forge became a wagon repair shop, the engine house a pattern shop and other buildings were remodelled to become foundries, blacksmith shops and fitting shops. The company owned a number of locomotives and several thousand wagons and all repairs to these were carried out at Aberaman. The photograph taken in the 1930s in the repair shop shows a pair of locomotive wheels mounted on a wheel lathe. The gentleman in the picture is Mr Reg Upton
Charles Vicary

116 The Gadlys Patent Fuel Works was erected shortly after the First World War by D.R. Llewellyn & Sons Ltd., as part of the company's coal mining undertaking in the Aberdare valley. The coal was collected from various collieries and was washed on the Gadlys site. Production capacity was about 500 tons a day and this included both ovoid and rectangular briquettes. The photograph shows the screens and the briquetting plant. To the left of the screens, off the photograph, is the power house which still stands today. The enterprise was short lived and closed in the late 1920s   *Douglas Williams*

117 The photograph of the Phurnacite Plant at Abercwmboi was taken in 1956, when there were three batteries of ovens in operation, producing about 350,000 tonnes of patent fuel. The growing nation wide demand for the high quality briquettes led to the building of four more batteries at intervals until the mid 1970s. About 800 men were now employed and production had risen to over 800,000 tonnes. However, in the 1980s there was growing local opposition to the pollution caused by the aging Dicticoke ovens and there was disagreement about the introduction of alternative methods of manufacture. The works, except for a small Ancit plant closed in 1990 and the ovens have since been dismantled. In the foreground of the picture is one of the settling ponds of the adjacent power station

118 The decline of coalmining, Aberdare's basic industry, in the 1920s threw vast numbers of men out of work and hundreds were forced to leave in search of work elsewhere. In the photograph taken on 26th March 1928, the two young men with suitcases are Jimmy Jones (left) and Haydn Campbell (right). They were leaving Aberdare under a government sponsored scheme to train as moulders in machine shops at Syston, near Leicester, and were the first young miners from South Wales to leave under such an arrangement. Relatives and local officials assembled at the low level station to see them off. The latter included the Chairman of the Council, Mr A.P. Thomas seen in the front row on Mr Campbell's left, and next to him, Mr G.L. Vickers, the manager of the Labour Exchange

Mrs A. Jones

119 Aberdare Cables came to Aberdare in 1937 when alternative employment to the declining coal industry was badly needed. Without a government subsidy, Sir George Usher, supported by Aberdare's M.P. Mr George Hall, established the factory on 24 acres of land on the Llwydcoed side of the river at Trecynon (see Vol. 1, Pl. 93). The original cables manufactured were paper impregnated power cables which had a worldwide distribution. Later telephone and telegraph cables were added. The photograph taken in the late 1950s shows one of the main shops with the machinery for spinning and winding the cables

Ken Davies

120 In 1570 Abercwmboi Isaf Farm formed part of the possessions of the Earl of Pembroke. By 1691 it had become one of the constituent farms of the Duffryn Aberdare Estate which was purchased by William Bruce in 1750 and subsequently passed by inheritance to Henry Austin Bruce, first Baron Aberdare of Duffryn. The farm which was also once known by the name of Troedrhiw-fer stood on the hillside now occupied by the Fernhill Estate and was a prominent landmark to be seen from the old Taff Vale Railway line

121 Today's 'Pant Farm' is a well known modern housing estate. The proper name of the land upon which it stands is Pantygerdinen which was once an ancient farm named in a manorial survey of 1630 as Tyr Pante y Gerdinen part of Tyr Pympynt. The tenement, then consisting of 20 acres, was occupied by a Nicholas Edwards. In the Nineteenth Century the farm was owned by Howell Williams who was a friend of Telynog (Thomas Evans) and assisted in collecting and publishing a volume of his works. The farm house, which is to be seen in this photograph was demolished around 1967 and was situated in the area now occupied by Derwent Drive and the new Infants School

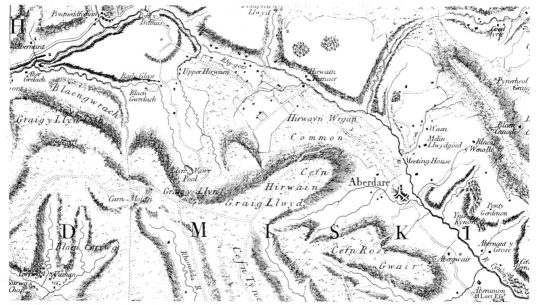

122   This is part of George Yates's 1799 map of Glamorgan on a scale of 1 inch to the mile and covers an area from Glyn Neath to Aberaman, which is beginning to be industrialised. The terminus of the Neath Canal at Abernant (Glyn Neath) is shown, as is Hirwaun Furnace and two small coal pits or iron mines about 1½ miles to the S.W. of it. The representation of relief is very generalised and the hachuring indicates only the degree of slope rather than the actual height of the land. In spite of the eccentricity and variety of spelling – Hirwaun for example – place names are easily recognisable. Llwydcoed Mill is shown and Hen Dy Cwrdd and St John's church appear although the symbol used indicates that the latter has a spire. Lower down the valley Aberaman House is indicated as being the residence of H. Lort instead of H. Lord (see also Vol. 1. Pl. 2(b)). This map and the next have not been reproduced to scale

123   This section of the 1875 25 inch to the mile Ordnance Survey map illustrates the semi-rural character of the upper part of Trecynon in the early 1870s. Except for the Llwyncelyn Inn and the adjoining Railway Inn (the latter not named), there are no houses along Cemetery Road, nor along the upper part of Windsor Street. Llewellyn Street, Iestyn Street, Cledwyn Terrace, the old Tegfan and the Social Service offices had yet to be built. The old farmhouse Tir Iorin surrounded by fields occupied the upper part of the site of the future Trefelin. The Dare and Aman branch of the Vale of Neath Railway crosses the map from its north western corner. Also shown are the mortuary chapel (Vol. 1, Pl. 28), the tollgate near the foot of Cwmdare Hill (Vol. 1, Pl. 117) and St Fagan's Church and School

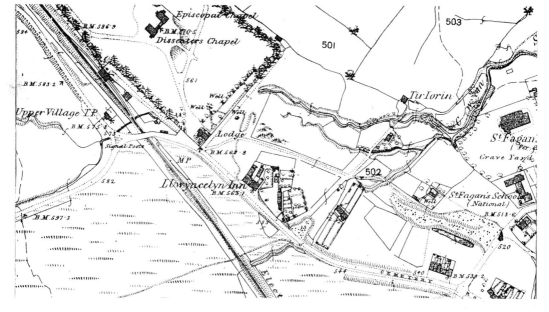

124 The average December rainfall for Aberdare based on the official observations at Nant Hir reservoir is 8.2ins (208mm). December 1979 recorded nearly double this amount – 15.8ins (401mm) and of this total, nearly 6ins (150mm) fell in a torrential downpour between mid-morning on Boxing Day and about midday on the 27th, when this photograph of the Trap Surgery was taken. It was this concentration of rainfall within a relatively short period which caused the Cynon to burst its banks and widespread flooding throughout the valley   *Tom Evans*

125 Sixty eight years earlier on December 18th 1911, a similar scene was recorded. Abernant Road at the Trap was under 3 feet of water and two small boys were swept into the river at Robertstown and drowned. A detailed breakdown of the rainfall has proved unobtainable but the total for December of that year was 17.8ins (over 450mm), the highest monthly total since records began in 1878 and it is reasonable to assume that a substantial proportion of this must have fallen between the 16th and 18th of the month. Note that in the picture two small cottages extend from the end wall of Nazareth Chapel (extreme right), across what is today the entrance to Cwmbach Road (compare Pl. 9 in OAM)

126 This winter scene taken probably in the late 1880s or early 1890s shows an unidentified part of the Aberdare Canal, completely frozen over. The intensity of the cold was obviously sufficient to produce a thickness of ice sufficient to support a man's weight. However in spite of the low temperature, the gentlemen disporting themselves nonchalantly in the picture, appear to scorn the wearing of overcoats   *Douglas Williams*

127 In February 1982 there occurred one of the heaviest and most prolonged snowfalls of recent years. Snow commenced falling about 8pm on Thursday 7th February and continued without a break until the early afternoon on Saturday the 9th. The main road to Cardiff was impassible until the following Monday and residential side streets such as Tudor Terrace, shown in the photograph, remained blocked for several days   *Douglas Williams*

128   This photograph was taken in about 1935 when the fire brigade in this area was run by the District Council and a new Ford-based fire engine was been delivered. Mr R.L. Berry (left) was the captain and he is seen here with Council Transport officials, Mr H. Hughes (right), who was Depot Superintendent, and the manager of the undertaking, Mr W.E. Richardson

129   The scene is Bwllfa Road, Cwmdare with Elim Chapel in the background. The photograph is a recent gift to the library and shows what is probably a water cart. A similar vehicle is shown in Pl. 33 in Vol. 1, taken at about the same time (about 1910) and about 250 yards away

130, 131 Toc H was the phonetic pronunciation of the letters T.H. the initials of Talbot House. It was founded in 1915 at Poperinghe in Belgium by the Rev. 'Tubby' Clayton as a recreation centre for soldiers of all ranks out of the line. Subsequently it developed into an interdenominational association for Christian social service. It was well represented in Aberdare in the interwar years with a main branch headquarters in High Street and subsidiary groups in Trecynon and Abernant. The Toc H Rovers (above) were affiliated to the Aberdare branch. The photograph taken in 1939 or 1940 included Mr Bert Berry, Rover Leader (centre seated) and on his right Mr Gwilym Davies, Assistant Leader. All had volunteered for National Service. Some years earlier, this photograph of the Aberdare branch (below) was taken outside St Elvans Church

132   The names of these 'Cwmbach Veterans' taken in 1932 are (L. to R., *sitting*) Alf Gough, Ivor Meredith, John Morris, Henry Obrey, Alf Lloyd, David Walters (*organiser*), John Hughes, Gabriel Morgan, William Jones, James Berry, Ben James, (*second row*) W.J Rees, F. Freeman, William Bevan, M. Jones, T. Harman, William Davies, David Williams, John Dew, M. Walter, D. Jones, David Lloyd, (*third row*) W. Harris, Henry Buchan, A. Marks, T. Palmer, D. Williams, James Parsons, D. Lewis, S. Grist, R. Evans, J. Jones, (*fourth row*) J. Currow, W. Rees, T. Evans, F. Gordon, T. Meredith, L. Thomas, J. Hughes, E. Lewis, David Davies, James Davies, (*fifth row*) James Williams, T. Walters, J. Williams, D. Jones, William James, T.H. Jones, W.H. Curnow, W. Jones, R. Jones, T. Walters, W. Maggs

133   In the early part of the war (about 1940) this group of Aberdarians training as stretcher bearers are photographed with their trainers and organisers in the front row, who include Dr Harry Banks and Dr J.M. Wilson. Also seen in the front row are the Vicar of Aberdare, the Rev. J. Wilfred Evans, and Mr P.G. Prosser (first right) of the 'Aberdare Leader'

134 Long before the country had a Minister for the Arts the town had a thriving Art Society. This was founded in 1938 by Mr E.J. Excell M.B.E. and originally met at the Cafe Mona, later moving to the Settlement. One of the original members was Mansel Jones who painted the cover illustrations for this book and Vol. 1. The Society disbanded on the outbreak of the Second World War, and was re-formed on the 19th February 1959 and held its first exhibition that same year when 54 paintings were shown. This photograph, taken on 22nd October 1961, shows the Society's President (Morys George Lyndhurst Bruce, 4th Baron Aberdare of Duffryn) previewing the 3rd, Exhibition. Left to right are G.I. John (Chairman), Idris Cole, Lord Aberdare, W. Haubenschmid (Treasurer) and E.J. Excell M.B.E. (Hon. Secretary)

135 Alderman Florence Rose Davies C.B.E., J.P., (1882–1958) was one of the leading women in public life in South Wales. She was born in Aberdare and lived there throughout her life. She was the daughter of William Henry Rees, a sorter at the Gadlys Tinplate Works, and Fanny, the eldest daughter of J. Lendon Berry who took this photograph. A school teacher who became a friend of Keir Hardie, she entered politics, represented the Gadlys Ward of the Aberdare U.D.C. and was the first woman Chairman of the Aberdare Education Committee. She successfully stood for the Glamorgan County Council in 1925 and was to become both its first woman Alderman and first woman Chairman. She unsuccessfully contested Honiton in the 1929 General Election being the first socialist to fight the seat. She became a Magistrate in 1920 and was created a Commander of the Most Excellent Order of the British Empire in 1952

136 Sam Jones & Co., Drapers and Millinery Specialists of Commerce House, Commercial Street, Aberdare was one of the town's leading fashion houses for over fifty years. More than half the staff seen in this group consist of women and young girls who would have been employed as dressmakers, window dressers and shop assistants. This photograph, taken in 1911, shows the staff of Commerce House enjoying a picnic at a local beauty spot – Abernant

137 The group of church women shown in this picture are probably members of the Mothers' Union of the Parish of Aberdare. This woman's society was formed nationally in 1876 to safeguard and strengthen christian family life, to uphold the lifelong vows of marriage and generally to play a proper part in the life of the church. Women were of course its backbone organizing bazaars, sewing guilds, jumble sales, cleaning the brass, washing choir vestments, keeping the church decorated with fresh flowers and many other necessary tasks. The only male to be seen in the group is the Revd. James Abraham Lewis, R.D., B.A., Vicar of Aberdare, from 1914 to 1931

138 (Top left) The famous name of Scale is usually associated with the iron industry. However, Thomas William Scale (1856–1938), the grandson of George Scale one of the founders of the Aberdare Iron Works at Lwydcoed, was a well known local Physician and Surgeon whose surgery and residence was at Gloster House, Whitcombe Street, Aberdare. Dr Scale trained at the Middlesex and Guys Hospital, London and at Durham University. He was a Member of the Royal College of Surgeons L.S.A. and L.R.C.P. (Lond.), and consulting surgeon to the Powell Duffryn Steam Coal Collieries under the Compensation Act and also assistant surgeon to the Cyfarthfa Iron and Steel works. He was for many years Aberdare's Registrar of Births, Deaths and Marriages. Dr Scale was a bachelor and left an estate of £75,000

139 (Above) The town's leading medical practitioner throughout the greater part of the nineteenth century was Dr David Davies J.P., F.R.C.S. He was born at Cwm-saerbren Farm, Rhondda, in 1821 and came to Aberdare in 1844 when the parish had a population of some 7000 and only one other doctor. Dr Davies became the Medical Officer of Health in 1854 a position which he held until his retirement in 1909. He also had his own medical practice which 'extended pretty generally over the whole parish'. He lived at Bryngolwg, Wind Street (since 1922 the Aberdare United Services Club) and his surgery was at the rear of the house. Dr Davies married a daughter of Joseph Coffin of Merthyr Tydfil and was Thomas Wayne's brother-in-law

140 William Simpson (1901–1990) studied Medicine at Edinburgh University (MB, ChB 1926, MD 1931), on the opposite bank of the Firth of Forth to Kirkcaldy, from whence he came. He came to Aberdare in 1929, joining a partnership of two with an assistant looking after 10,000 patients with many night calls. When younger, he was a keen rugby player and golfer. Apart from war service, he remained for the rest of his life in Aberdare, where he was greatly esteemed and respected by his patients, and now lies in St. Fagan's Churchyard, in the centre of the district in which he spent over 50 years in medical practice

141 The employment of women and of children under 10 years old underground had been illegal since 1842 though it took over 10 years for the practice to be eradicated. These women of Bwllfa Colliery in about 1870 are however surface workers, probably picking out stone and other unwanted substances from the coal just raised from the pit. It has been stated that the employment of women surface workers was not common in south Wales, especially in the 'new' pits that opened in the second half of the 1800s

142 Claimed to have been the first in the country, the 'Aberdare Leader's talking newspaper for the blind started in 1957 with an idea by the late Ron Sleeman, which was enthusiastically taken up by the paper's editor, Gwyn Prosser. Here seen in a recording seession are (left to right) Clayson Lovell, Gwyn Prosser, Elizabeth Mear (now Makin), Brian Selwyn, Jocelyn Prosser (now Britz), and Glyn Griffiths, all 'Leader' staff except Brian Selwyn. The newspaper is still produced, though with the demise of the Blind Institute multiple copies of the tape are sent to blind persons' homes, rather than played back to an assembly   *Mrs E. Makin*

143 It is October 1945 and the war is over. For the young men still in the RAF, such as Flying Officer T.L. Taylor from Broniestyn Tce, flying had suddenly become enjoyable, and if an error in navigation on a training mission from RAF Chivenor to a range in the Bristol Channel results in his seeing Aberdare from the air for the first time – what a good thing he had a camera with him! Taken from above Abernant, the picture shows St Elvans Church just below centre, with the low level (left) and high level stations at the bottom. The wingtip of F/O Taylor's Mosquito FB6 can also be seen   *T.L. Taylor*

144 On the 20 June 1910, the Aberaman Horse Show and Agricultural Society held its 9th Annual Exhibition at Aberaman Park. Its President that year was Edward Curre, of Itton Court, Chepstow, after whose family Curre Street in Aberaman is named. The Society awarded £250 in prizes and 5 silver cups, and there were classes for Hackneys, heavy horses, Yeomanry, jumping, trotting and galloping as well as cattle and sheep. This photograph shows the Society's Committee. Its Chairman was J. Morgan (seated centre?) the Vice Chairman A.L. Morgan (seated front row third from left), butcher of 55 Lewis Street, Aberaman. The Secretary was Tom Rees (seated 5th from left) the Landlord of the Broad Oak Inn, 6 Lewis Street, Aberaman. Amongst those in the group are W. Druce (2nd right back row) and Harry Cohen (seated on grass)

145 The Aberdare and District Chamber of Trade and Commerce was established in 1880 but had ceased to be active by 1893. It was re-founded in 1909 and its first President was Illtyd Williams of Compton House. This photograph was taken at the Café Mona, probably at the Chamber's Annual Dinner, in 1960. Its President that year was Mr Maldwyn Jones J.P. (seated centre), a Builder's Merchant. Its membership in 1960 reflects the prosperity of the commercial life of the town at that time and readers will recognize many familiar faces once seen behind the counters of long gone shops and businesses

146   During the 1912 royal visit to the South Wales valleys, King George V and Queen Mary were shown the interior of a 'typical' colliers cottage in Bute Street (See Pl. 3 to 7 in OAM) and were also greeted by the 'establishment' of the town and presented with a Loyal Address by the High Constable, Joseph Henry Powell. This splendid photograph shows the reception party of perhaps slightly apprehensive local worthies asembled in the park for the cermony just prior to the arrival of the Royal Daimler. Amongst those on the platform are the Vicar, the Rev. C.A.H. Green D.D. (left in mortar board and bands), Col.T. Phillips, Clerk of the Council (with wig), J.H. Powell (in robes) and on his left is D. Davies J.P. Cwmbach Chairman of the Council. Next to him is Rees Llewellyn (holding cane), the Chairman of the Bwllfa and Merthyr Dare Steam Colleries (1891) Ltd

147 This photograph, by J.L. Berry of a working class woman wearing a cap and canvas apron, shows her washing clothes by hand. The hot water for the wash would have been boiled over the kitchen fire and carried to the large wooden tub in which she pounds, scrubs and wrings the clothes by hand, operations which involved considerable physical effort. In a slightly earlier period the water would also first have to be brought from the nearest pump, spout or stream. Many married and unmarried females became washer-women, working from their own homes, in order to supplement the family income. The canary in the cage which hangs from the ceiling was a common feature in working class houses at the end of the 19th century

148 In 1852 the Aberdare Market Company, whose Directors were local landowners and businessmen, was granted exclusive rights by Parliament to set up a cattle market and slaughterhouse in the town. This was in the buildings opposite the entrances to the present day market. Some years later a bigger slaughterhouse was built on the site now occupied by the swimming pool. Cattle and sheep auctions were held there and this is a photograph of the last one, held in the 1950s. Among those in the group around the auction ring is Mr Jack Williams of the Werfa, a well known descendant of the family which had owned that farm since the 17th century   *Hans Hoyer*

149   After the disastrous fire at Aberdare Hospital in 1929 (See Vol. 1, Pl. 36 and 37) the building was renovated and re-equipped and officially re-opened in April 1933. The following year the former Prime Minister, The Rt. Hon David Lloyd George O.M., M.P. made a tour of the Cynon Valley which included an 'informal' visit to the new hospital. Before leaving 'L. G.' was photographed with senior hospital staff and other officials. *Front row* (L. to R.); Dr Isaac Banks, W.J. Hodges, Mrs Llewellyn, D.J. Davies, D. Lloyd George, R.J. Brace, Dame Margaret Lloyd George, Mrs C. Kenshole, G.H. Hall, A.W. Humphreys, Dr Martin Jones. *Second row*: W.R. Morgan, John Lewis, Mrs G.H. Hall, Mrs T. Phillips, E. Stonelake, Sister Thomas, Emrys Evans, W.J. Edwards, Tom Lucas, Arthur Harris. *Third row*: Tom Rees, John James, Ivor Bryant, Mrs D.J. Davies, Mrs A.W. Humphreys, Mrs Ben Brace, Mrs W.J. Edwards, Glen George, Henry Rees, (inset) Matron L. Richards

150   The history of Fedw Hir itself can be traced back to medieval times and is being recorded elsewhere. Part of its story however, is that in 1931 the land was acquired by the Council as the site for an isolation hospital for cases of small-pox. Later the hospital was used as an open residential school for children suffering from rheumatism and certain other diseases. Then in 1959 it became a recovery hospital and later a geriatric unit. Despite several changes of use it was still designated for use as a small-pox hospital until comparatively recently to serve the Aberdare and Merthyr Tydfil areas should the need arise. It had accommodation for 72 beds. The hospital closed a few years ago and the premises are now used by the Merthyr Tydfil and Aberdare Groundwork Trust

151 The Salvation Army was planted in Aberdare by Mother Shepherd in 1878 (see OAM, Pl. 33). Two barracks were soon established, one in High Street and the other in Regent Street, Aberaman. For decades, Salvationists were a familiar sight in the town and they may be particularly remembered for the outdoor band recitals, especially on Sunday evenings and for their dauntless excursions into the public houses on Saturday nights to sell the *War Cry*. Few customers refused to buy a copy. Two lady members of the Army are seen in the photograph taken in Aberaman, probably in the late 19th century

152 After its formation in 1895, the Aberdare Urban District Council became responsible for local fire services. The newly formed brigade consisted entirely of volunteers who received remuneration only for the time spent in attending fires. The 1911 photograph shows the Aberdare Brigade in full dress uniform with certificates and a cup indicating that they had won first and second prizes in the South Wales District Annual Competition in Newport in that year. The photograph is taken, like so many others of the period, outside the entrance to Aberdare Hospital. When the hospital burned down in 1929, two of those in this picture were to lose their lives – Mr R. Jenkins (3rd from left, 2nd row) and Mr W.J. Pink (extreme right in the front row) (Vol. 1. Pls. 36 and 37)

153 Many of the photographs in this book were taken by the late Glyn Davies ('Glyn the Co-op'). His vast collection of photographs was given to the Library after his death and will give pleasure to many generations to come. He believed in the merit of putting a human figure in his compositions or, occasionally his bicycle – see Pl. 48. Here he sits on the western extremity of Graig Rhiw Ddu, overlooking his beloved Aberdare

154 A view of Aberdare dating from before 1890 taken from the top of Ty Draw road over the fields on which the Girls Comprehensive School stands. On the left, three rows of cottages, Abernant Place, Abernant Row and Cefn Place (known collectively as Tai'r Ynys) stand where the Magistrates Court and Fire Station now are. Nazareth Chapel, now part of Harcros, is conspicuous to the left of centre, and to the left of that is the Commercial Hotel and to its right at a little distance can be seen the long low roof of the High Level station. The chimneys of many collieries and works can also be seen

155 This is an aerial photograph of Aberdare town centre taken in 1929. About half the buildings in the bottom left quarter have gone. These include the flat-roofed Dare Valley Motors garage, and to the left of it the Rock brewery (see OAM Pl. 66). Compare the unplanned jumble of buildings with the Victorian grid-iron layout of Maesydre (top right). In the top left quarter, buildings since demolished include Ty Mawr and its outbuildings (see Pl. 8 and 9). The Vestry Hall (behind the Town Hall), St Mair's Church (see OAM Pl. 25), the Heathcock and the Bridgend (see Pl. 47). In the centre of the bottom right quarter can be seen the row of cottages which stood where the Rex cinema was later built

Aerofilms

156 Crawshay's Tower, now only a pile of stones, was 30 feet high and 12 feet internal diameter. It had three rooms one above another each with a fireplace. It was built between 1846 and 1848 by Francis Crawshay (see Pl. 86 and 106) and in view of his well-known eccentricity it is perhaps pointless to speculate why it was built. It is often said that it was intended as a refuge for the Crawshays in time of industrial strife, but a moment's thought will reveal the absurdity of this theory   *J.F. Mear*

157 A view of old Greenfach taken from the railway to Cwmdare not later than 1907. The pine ends of 4 short rows of cottages which extend to the river Dare are on the right. The two nearest the camera are Dare Place and the next row is Dare Street. Next to Siloa is Chapel Street. These 4 rows are separated from the cottages on the left (Gadlys Row) by Green Street

ABERDARE LOOKING DOWN THE VALLEY.

158 This photograph was taken (probably from an upper window of Park School) before 1934, when the stack at the Boys County School was taken down. The stacks on the left at Gadlys have also gone, as has Carmel Chapel, centre of picture. The white cottage (bottom centre) stood where the entrance to the Ambulance Station now is, but it was one of the properties demolished when the Coliseum was built

J.F. Mear

159 Though captioned Lletyshenkin very little can be seen in this picture of that part of Cwmbach, which was on the right in the far distance behind Capel Bryn Seion. To the right of centre are coal trucks probably on the Cwmbach branch line and to the left the ventilation stack of High Duffryn Colliery. The whitewashed Gnoll farm can be seen high on the left. This is a picture postcard which was still on sale in the mid 1950s

Llettyshenkin, Cwmbach.

160 The two small settlements (now disappeared) in the Cwm were Cwm Place near the Dare Viaduct seen in Vol. 1, Pl. 110, and Cwm, consisting firstly of three houses (one or two more were added later), of which the largest (above) was nearest the town. Standing opposite the river footbridge which is still there, this house was built on the site of the original Cwm farm and was still occupied in 1871 by a Rees, one of the family associated with Cwm farm for at least 100 years before that

161 Taken before 1915 when the trolley buses (Pl. 26) were put into service, this photograph shows Abernant Road before the villas were built on the left side of the road. The entrance to Abernant house (now the hospital) is on the left, and the first building on the right was the Aberdare Steam Laundry, built in 1891

162 The Aberdare Rugby Football Team 1903–04. This was a highly successful season for the home team in that they won 21 out of 24 matches played at the Ynys. *Back row*: L. to R.: O.J. Hughes, Chairman; S. Bowen, J. Richards, A. Davies, J. Thomas, R. Harris, G. John, W. Bevan, F. Lewis, A. Strong, Secretary. *Middle row*: E. Evans, D. Thomas, J. Jones, F. Lucimore, D. Jones, A. Morgan, G. Key. *Front row*: W. Morgan, E. Jones. D. Jones, the captain, holding the ball in the second row gained 13 caps for Wales between 1902 and 1906 and was a member of the Welsh side which triumphed over New Zealand in 1905. W. Morgan in the front row is almost certainly Billy Morgan, the brother of the legendary Dr Teddy Morgan (Vol. 1 Pl. 86a), who was himself capped for Wales in the Scotland match of 1910

163 Handball, 'chware-pêl', was an old Glamorgan game which was revived in the 19th century, particularly in the eastern part of the county. Its vogue in Aberdare and Llanwynno is mentioned in Glanffrwyd's 'Hanes Plwyf Llanwynno'. It was played by 2 or 4 players striking a leather bound ball with the flat of a hand usually against the pine end wall of a public house until one of the players failed to return it, whereupon points were awarded to his opponent. In Cwmbach the favourite location was the gable end of the old Cooperative store opposite the Lifeboat Inn. The medal shown here is in the proud possession of the recipient's nephew, Mr George Lloyd of Cwmdare   *Douglas Williams*

164 Cwmaman Tug-of-War Team – Winners of the Championship of South Wales at Mountain Ash, September 1913: Tug-of-War was another traditional sport which became popular in the later 19th and the earlier 20th centuries for the same reasons as handball. In this case all that was necessary was a suitable rope, a field and the requisite number of strong men. The team members are the gentlemen in white pullovers. *2nd row* L. to R.: J. Darch; W.R. Darch; J. Jones; H.J. Charley; S. Henton; P. Hext; G.H. Morgan (Secretary). *Front Row*: W. Banner; J. Hurley; Councillor W. Jones (Treasurer); T.J. Howells (Capt); D. Edwards (Chairman); T. Daniel; W. Thomas. *Inset*: W.H. Heppell, M.E. President – General Manager of Cwmaman Collieries

165 Soccer became popular in South Wales in the 1880s and there was a remarkable upsurge of enthusiasm for the game in the middle of the first decade of the 20th century. The Aberdare Crescents were one of four teams in Aberdare town itself; there were in addition at least another eight from the outlying villages and districts. They were the winners of the Aberdare and District 1904–5, 1905–6, 1906–7 and they also won the 'Weekly Post' League Championship for 1906–7. The photograph taken in 1907 shows the team and officials. The team members in striped shirts are: *Middle Row* L. to R: D. Pritchard; J. Davies; W. Phillips; A. Jackson; T. Penry. *Front Row*: G. King; W. Thomas; J. Eynon; J. Lewis (Capt); D. Williams; T. Behenna; S. Probert

No. 239   Share Certificate.   5 Shares.

Aberdare Athletic Club, Limited.

Incorporated under "The Companies Acts, 1908 to 1917."

CAPITAL   - -   £10,000,

Divided into 10,000 Shares of One Pound each.

This is to Certify that *Wm John Harris* of *29 Queen St, Cwmdare, Aberdare* is the Registered Proprietor of *Five* fully-paid Shares of One Pound each, numbered *1033* to *1037* inclusive, in the above-named Company, subject to the Memorandum and Articles of Association and Regulations of the said Company.

Given under the Common Seal of the said Company, this *3rd* day of *Nov* 1920

W Cas Jones   Secretary.

Wm Llewellyn
Illtyd Williams   Directors.

N.B.—This Certificate must accompany any transfer of the above Shares lodged

166 In 1920 the Aberdare Athletic Club was formed as a limited company with an authorized capital of £10,000, most of which was raised locally through the issue of £1 shares. The leading instigators were W.M. Llewellyn, colliery proprietor of Bwllfa House and Illtyd Williams, a well-known Aberdare business man. They were appointed directors of the new club. A ground was laid out at the Ynys and the Aberdare Athletic Football Club, whose colours were claret and light blue, was admitted to the 3rd Division in 1921 where they remained until 1927 (see Vol. 1, Pl. 156)   *K. Harris*

167 The Aberdare Town Tennis Club was in existence for some 80 years before it ceased to function in the 1970s. This photograph was taken about 1920 outside its headquarters at Robertstown. *Back Row* L. to R: Unknown; Idris Jones; Donald Phillips; Arthur Thomas; Unknown; Harry Williams; Dan Davies; Norman Berry; Unknown. *Third Row*: D. Beynon Jones; Gertie Francis; Tom Roderick; John Evans?; Mary Jones; Tom James; Jack Burge; Willie Hodges. *Second Row*: Frank Hodges; Mrs D. Parry; Mabs Burge; Rene Martin; D. Herbert Davies; Mrs D. Beynon Jones; Cliff Thomas; Mrs Harry Williams; Mrs Alec Cameron; Mrs I.E. Thomas; W.D. Morris. *Front Row*: David Parry; Cissie Jones; Edgar Jones; Phyllis Burge; Alec Cameron; Mrs Mattie Thomas; Russell Phillips; Mrs Dan Davies; Edgar Hodges. *In front, sitting on the ground*: Minnie Tay; Phyllis Harrison   *Mrs P. Harrison Roderick*

168 The Cwmdare Welfare Cricket Club was formed shortly after the opening of the Welfare Pavilion in 1926. This photograph was taken about 1950. *Back Row* L. to R: Arthur Morgan; Graham Andrews; Derek Phillips; Dick Williams; Howard Lane: a visitor. *Front Row*: Gwyn Morgan; Ken Lewis; Islwyn Samuels; Trevor Stonelake; Dai Jones. *Seated on the ground*: Teddy Sly. Gwyn Morgan is currently the EEC's ambassador to Thailand   *Trevor Stonelake*

169 Three well known golfing personalities are seen here. L to R – Rufus Evans, Dai Rees and Mansel Williams. The occasion was a Complimentary Dinner held in November 1949 to mark the promotion of the Aberdare Golf Team to Division 1 in the Glamorgan County League, the success of two of its members in reaching the semi-final of the Welsh Amateur Championship and the achievement of the Aberdare Golf Club's honorary member, Dai Rees (Vol. 1, Pl. 86c) in winning for the third time the 'News of the World' Match Play Championship. In the immediate post-war years Rufus Evans and Mansel Williams formed a highly successful partnership in National and League events, winning amongst other achievements the Gold Medal in the Victory Cup, All Wales Foursomes Championships in 1950. Between them they won the Individual Championships of the Aberdare Club 21 times between 1947 and 1971   *Mrs Nest Evans*

ABERDARE MUSICAL ASSOCIATION.

PRESIDENT,
THOMAS WAYNE, Esq.

VICE-PRESIDENT,
WILLIAM S. CLARK, Esq.

SECRETARIES,
GEORGE ASHCROFT, Esq.
JAMES SHERBORNE, Esq.

TREASURERS.
T. B. POWELL, Esq., Brecon Old Bank.
THOMAS DAVIES, Esq., West of England Bank.

MUSICAL DIRECTORS,
FREDERICK HELMORE, Esq., CHOIR-MASTER
to H.R.H. Prince Albert.
EDWARD LAWRANCE, Esq., of the Conservatorium of Music, Leipzig.

The objects of the Association are as follows:—

1st. To furnish a pleasant Musical Evening every week, when will be practised Vocal and Instrumental Compositions, comprising Operatic Choruses, Oratorios, Motets, Madrigals, Glees, German Part-songs, Overtures, Sonatas, &c., &c.

2nd. To give instruction to Ladies and Gentlemen in Part-music suited for the Drawing-room.

3rd. By meeting in numbers under the able direction of Mr. Helmore an excellent opportunity will be afforded of studying compositions of the great Masters, without which study a thorough appreciation of their beauties cannot be realized.

4th. It is proposed occasionally to hold Soirees and Musical Conversaziones or Drawing-room Concerts.

Weekly Meetings of the Association will be held in the Assembly Room, Market House, on Tuesdays. The First Meeting will take place on Tuesday, the 15th October, instant, at Seven o'clock in the evening. The Assembly Room will be carpeted and comfortably warmed and seated.

The Season will commence on the 15th of October, and terminate at Easter.

TICKETS FOR THE SEASON :—

To admit one £1 1 0
Ditto each additional member of the
    same family 0 10 6

Tickets may be had on application to the President, Vice-president, Secretaries, or Treasurers.
Aberdare, October 2nd, 1861.

TEMPERANCE HALL,
ABERDARE.

JANUARY 9th, 1862.

Under the special patronage of

H. A. BRUCE, ESQ., M.P.

A GRAND MUSICAL AND LITERARY
SOIREE

WILL be given at the above HALL on the above date, by Mr. Le COUNT DUPONT DE NEMOURS. Chevalier of many Orders, London ex-special Correspondent of the *Moniteur Universel*, official journal of the French empire, Vice-President of the Imperial Society of Archivists of France, &c.,

ASSISTED BY

THE ABERDARE RIFLE CORPS BAND,
THE ABERAMAN RIFLE CORPS BAND,
THE MOTNTAIN ASH GLEE PARTY,
Mr. JOHN THOMAS, of the TREAMAN CHORAL SOCIETY,
Mr. J. MORGAN, Pianist,
Mr. DAVID EVANS, and a number of the most talented Artistes of the neighbourhood.

A FRENCH ORATION

Will be given by M. DUPONT DE NEMOURS.
Also an ENGLISH TRANSLATION by Mr. A. M.
An ADDRESS (in Welsh) by the Rev. S. DAVIES.
OPERA.—Sacred Music by Meyerbeer, Donizetti, Rossini, and by the first modern composers.
Solo and Chorus by the MOUNTAIN ASH GLEE PARTY.
Songs, Duetts, Trios, Quartetts, Catches, &c., by the ORCHESTRAL ASSOCIATION.

Admission :—Reserved seats, 2s.; Front seats, 1s. 6d.; Second ditto, 1s.; Back ditto, 6d.

Tickets to be obtained of Mr. THOMAS, Druggist; Mr. EVANS, Druggist; Mr. ORCHARD, Mill-street; and at the Office of this paper.

---

170   The town of Aberdare was widely known in literary and musical circles as the 'Athens of Wales' because of the many cultural activities held here throughout the nineteenth-century. These interesting advertisements, taken from the pages of *The Aberdare Times* and dating from the early 1860s, are given as an example of the rich diversity of events held here during the century. The Assembly Room, where the Musical Association met, was part of the Market Hall (now the Market Tavern) built in 1853. Patrons were assured that this would be 'carpeted and comfortably warmed and seated.' The President and Vice President were respectively an Iron Master and the Marquis of Bute's mineral agent, and one of the Secretaries (Sherborne) was an Aberdare Silversmith and Jeweller

171 One of the leading groups of local theatrical players were the Aberdare Teachers Dramatic Society. This photograph was taken in 1948 when the Society performed Oscar Wilde's 'Lady Windermere's Fan' at the Coliseum Theatre. The members of the cast were: *seated*, L. to R. Miss Vi Jones, Miss Gwyneth Evans, Miss Mary Williams, Miss Ivy Morgan, Miss Dorothy Callaghan (Lady Windermere), Miss Edith Evans (Mrs Erlyn) Miss Fenella Tippett, Miss Blodwen Powell. *Standing* Miss Rowena Wallace, Mr Edwin Davies, Mr Gwilym Evans, Mr Arthur Thomas (Lord Windermere), Miss Winifred Rees (Producer), Mr Ben Davies (Lord Darlington), Mr Meirion Lewis, Mr D.R.C. Owen, Mr William James

172 The Trecynon Amateur Dramatic Society was founded in 1909 but had no permanent playhouse until 1931. In that year the brothers Sir David Llewellyn and W.M. Llewellyn of Bwllfa made the Society a gift of a spot of land and an old locomotive shed erected on it which had once housed engines belonging to the Gadlys Iron & Coal Co. With the aid of a bank loan, guaranteed by W.M. Llewellyn, the former loco shed was converted into a theatre – Aberdare's famous 'Little Theatre' which celebrated its Jubilee last year. The Theatre's Architect and Builder was Councillor Tysull Davies J.P. This photograph shows the opening ceremony being performed by Miss Elizabeth Llewellyn (Sir D.R.'s sister) who is seen unlocking the door with a golden key

173 Eisteddfodau have been held in Aberdare since 1820 and the very first 'National' Eisteddfod was held here in 1861. This important cultural festival has been held here on two occasions since, in 1885 and 1956. This photograph records a part of the Proclamation Ceremony held at the Park in 1955 in which the Eisteddfod trumpeters signal that an Eisteddfod is about to be proclaimed and that Aberdare is the chosen venue

174 In addition to the customary competitions in singing and elocution a varied programme of concerts, plays and exhibitions of fine arts and crafts were held at Aberdare during the National Eisteddfod in 1956. Amongst the highlights of the week were performances of works given by the London Symphony Orchestra and other artistes. This photograph, taken in the Pavilion at the Park on the 9th August, is of a concert of choral works by Bach, and David de Lloyd. The Orchestra and National Eisteddfod Choir (T.R. James Chorus Master, were conducted by A. Meredith Davies. The two female soloists seen here are Helen Watts (right) and Norma Morgan of Aberdare, who later became a professional singer

175 In 1930 a fete was held in the town to raise money in support of the Aberdare General Hospital following the fire. The fete was a success and became an annual event. This romantic photograph was taken during the 6th Annual fete held at the Aberdare Park from the 8th–15th September 1935. Events included a military band, jazz bands, aquatic sports, an Eisteddfod, dancing competitions, sheep dog trials, Brass band competitions, variety shows, dancing on the green and community singing. The entire park was turned into a 'Fairy land amongst the trees' by brilliant lighting effects of which the main attraction was the lake and bandstand, seen in this picture, which was gaily illuminated with fairy lights, multi-coloured lamps and giant floodlights. The crowd on the final day of this particular fete numbered 10,000

176 This photograph is included primarily as a record of the Rock Baths, once one of the town's favourite places of recreation in summer. The baths were opened in 1938 and closed, despite protests, in 1975. When they were demolished a symbolic wreath was laid on the remains of the pool. There was once an active swimming club in the town. This was formed in 1924 and at one time had over 500 members. At that time people used to swim in the park lake. The club's activities included an annual Gala and its water polo team are seen here at the Rock Baths in the 1964 event. The players are left to right (front row) Hywel Morris, Brian Loveridge, Cyril Edevane and Colin Sexton. (back row) John Jones, ?, Ron Arthur, Les Venn, Bev Morris, Phillip Verrier and Jim McCarthy (Pool Manager)

177 The popular culture of jazz-bands developed during the strikes and depressions in the years between the two world wars and had their hey-day in 1926. They were not only an escape from everyday realities but boosted morale and asserted collective values. The photograph of this group and their supporters seen parading along Cardiff Road, Aberaman was taken during the period of the General Strike in 1926. The shop in the background is that of E. Short, Fruiterer

178 A photograph of the famous Aberdare Town Band which achieved a world record in 1906 when it won 20 first, 3 second and 3 third prizes in competitions during the course of that year. Equally famous was its bandmaster, from 1906 to 1930, Jesse Manley (holding baton) Composer, Music teacher and Adjudicator. The foreman boiler-maker at the Gadlys Works, Manley was associated with band music in Aberdare for over 40 years founding the Ysguborwen Colliery Band which he also conducted. He was originally a cornet player and had been professional conductor of 9 bands in Scotland as well as an adjudicator of band contests at the Crystal Palace and Belle Vue, Manchester. He died in 1933, aged 70, and is buried in the old cemetery Aberdare where his grave is to be seen inscribed with a music stave and treble clef

179 The 'Rex', Aberdare's Super-de-luxe Cinema, owned by William E. Willis, was opened at Easter time (April) 1939. It contained 1700 seats and was the last word in 'comfort and colour'. On the occasion of the opening there were large queues outside all day despite glorious sunshine. The first two films shown were 'Three Loves has Nancy' starring James Gaynor, Robert Montgomery and Franchot Tone, and 'The Garden of the Moon' with Pat O'Brien. The cinema's great attraction was the celebrated Compton Theatrone Organ (see next Pl.). The Rex continued to show films (including such exciting innovations as 'CinemaScope') regularly until 1974. It was demolished in 1990

180 The Compton Theatrone Organ at the Rex was a popular feature of a visit to that theatre. In art-deco style the organ, the first of its kind in Wales, had 2 consols and 500 valves, and would rise out of the floor beneath the stage. Its glass surround was illuminated by 140 interior strip lights which changed colour automatically. A month after the opening of the cinema, Reginald Fortt gave a two hour recital in aid of Bethel Chapel, Gadlys and pronounced the organ 'a peach'. The cinema's resident organist (seen here) was Blaengarw born Walford James who had been organist at the Astoria Cinema, Bournemouth. His signature tune was 'It's in the Air.' He gave three performances daily

181 The Cosy Cinema in Market Street was opened by William Haggar in August 1915 and provided a welcome escape from the hardships of war. This large advertisement, dating from 1936, for the famous Chaplin film 'Modern Times' was hand-painted by a local artist, Mr Jack Meredith, who later became assistant manager at the Rex. The hoarding stood opposite the Cosy on ground (once the Market cattle-yard and pound) which had been used by visiting fit-up theatres and entertainers from the 1840s and where William Haggar himself first exhibited. The Cosy provided a Workmen's matinee on Wednesdays at 10.15 am and one for children on Saturdays at the same time and promised 'powerful supporting programmes'

182 Victor Freed was a well known local business man who specialised in the sale of furniture, pianos and musical instruments. His firm was founded around 1900 and had premises at Nos. 1 and 60 Cardiff Street and 7 Market Street (the old Cosy Cinema). In the 1920s the firm promoted a Piano Accordion Band (seen here) which played under the direction of Billy Thomas. The accordion band was a concert group which frequently raised money for charity. One of its popular concert pieces was an arrangement of Suppé's Poet and Peasant Overture and the band's programmes often opened with this work. Billy Thomas, a well known musician, was a butcher with Dewhurst's. He was organist at Ynysllwyd Chapel, Aberaman, and conductor of the Coliseum Operatic Society. He also sometimes played the Rex cinema organ

183 Modelled on the Salvation Army the Anglican Church Army was founded in the slums of London in 1882. A Corps of the Llandaff Church Army was formed in Aberdare on the 8th January 1888 under the command of Capt. Wine. Its meetings were held at an old saw mill in Gloucester Street and the first congregation numbered 700. The Army had its own brass band and held regular church parades. Its officers were evangelical and this caravan was designed to tour the parish and take the word to the people

184   The tea-party was one of the great social institutions of church and chapel life. In the Bachelor's tea-party, it was the custom that the young unmarried males in the congregation carried out all the functions connected with such an event – preparing the 'eatables', acting as cutters, door keepers and general supervisors. The spotless white aprons worn by the smartly turned out young men of Siloa Chapel, Aberdare suggest that the repast had not yet taken place. This party was held in May 1908 during a period of religious fervour. The proceedings ended with an evening concert with songs and recitations which was presided over by the Pastor, the Rev. D. Silyn Evans

185   Siloa Welsh Congregational Chapel was founded in 1842 and is unique in that it had only three ministers down to 1964. These were the Rev. David Price (1843–1878), the Rev. D. Silyn Evans (1880–1930) and the Rev. R. Ivor Parry (1933–1964). This photograph showing Mr Parry (seated centre) and the Siloa Diaconate was taken in June 1933, on the occasion of his ordination as Minister. (Back) L. to R.: David Stephens, William Davies M.E., Thomas Davies, James Williams, (Brecon Meat). (Front): L. to R.: Ivor J. John, R.J. Evans (whose father was the Rev. D. Silyn Evans), the Rev. R. Ivor Parry M.A., John Zachariah and Jacob Phillips

186 The Richard Bowen Jenkins Memorial Hall, in Seymour Street, was erected in 1895 to commemorate the 10 years of ministry of the Rev. W. Bowen Jenkins M.A., as Vicar of the Parish of Aberdare. The Hall and adjoining Church club premises cost £3200. It was built of Ruabon red brick by Messrs. Bowers & Co., Hereford and its architect was Mr Wakely of Merthyr Tydfil. The premises contained a dance hall, gymnasium, billiard, table tennis, reading and refreshment rooms, Vicar's Parlour and Steward's accommodation. Neglected by the parochial authorities the 'Mem.' fell into disrepair and was demolished in 1989

187 An unfamiliar view of one of Aberdare's best known landmarks – the weather-cock of St. Elvan's church. This particular specimen, which is made of brass, is 180 feet from the ground, but has descended from its perch on a few occasions since it was set up for restoration, regilding and to facilitate repairs to the steeple. The three boys seen with this unusual 'plaything' are Vicary Miles (sitting), behind him, Tom Morris and on his left, Charles Vicary. The photograph was taken in 1924 when the steeple was being repaired and the weather-cock was found to be 'out of order' and had to be sent away for re-adjustment   *Charles Vicary*

188, 189   The enlarged Abernant House (above) was the residence of the ironmaster Richard Fothergill. On St. David's Day 1892 it became a Theological College – St. Michael's and All Angels – for the training of candidates for Holy Orders in the then four Welsh Dioceses. One of the rooms (seen below) of the house was converted into a chapel and furnished accordingly. The photograph also shows the detail of the elegant decoration of the room as it was during the period Richard Fothergill resided there. St. Michael's College removed to Llandaff in 1907 and is still in existence there today. Its foundation at Aberdare, one hundred years ago, is commemorated in the name College Street   *R.J. Evans*

190 On a June day in 1904 a little boy from Aberaman decided to go off with his hoop instead of going back to school after dinner. He never returned. Public meetings were held to organise search parties and these were addressed by Mr Tom W. Griffiths, Solicitor, (left) and Mr C.B. Stanton, Miners' Agent (right). A bloodhound was brought by Colonel Joynson of Tachbrooke Mallory, Leamington, (centre?) to assist in the search. Two days later as another mass meeting was being held on Victoria Square, the news came that the body of the boy had been found in a pool of the Cynon near Aberaman station. His hoop was nearby on the bank

191 This portrait states on the back that it was taken at Aberdare on the 24th of November 1856 and is included in this book because it is the oldest known photograph connected with Aberdare. The original is an 'Ambrotype', a wet collodion process invented in 1848. The identity of the sitter is not known, but he is thought to be a member or friend of the Williams family of the Werfa, Abernant, from whence the photograph originated. Has anyone out there an older Aberdare photograph than this? *E.G. Williams*

192 This document, dated 1873, reveals that Edwin Spraggs paid a fee of £5 to his union (The Amalgamated Association of Miners) for learning the trade of coal-cutting. The Association was then at the height of its powers, having won a dispute in the beginning of that year, and in 1871. However, a decline in trade union support started in 1874, and in 1875, at a time of falling sales, the Association was not able to resist a cut in wages. The terms of settlement of that dispute led to the introduction of the famous 'sliding scale'

193 It always seems improper to take photographs of a funeral and this picture taken with the former Boys' County School in the background is therefore unusual. It seems likely that the photographer hid his camera until the hearse and principal mourners had passed. The custom of mourners walking to the cemetery behind the hearse was still being observed locally in the late 1950s, but only in the case of miners who were killed in work   *J.F. Mear*

STATUE OF CARADOG, ABERDARE.

194, 195 The story of how Griffith Rhys Jones (Caradog) took the combined choirs known as the South Wales Choral Union to a great victory at the Crystal Palace in 1873 will never be forgotten in Aberdare as long as Caradog remains to command our attention in Victoria Square (above). This picture is also a reminder – that Caradog is no longer in his original place (see Pl. 15), having been moved when alterations were carried out as part of a Civic Trust scheme in 1962. The medal (below) was presented to each member of the successful choir by Richard Fothergill, local ironmaster and M.P., and is the prized possession of a descendant of one of the recipients

196 Thought to have been taken at the Golf Club, the nature of this jollification remains unknown. On the left is Wyndham G. Williams of the Werfa with his son, Edward, third from left. Third from right is the late Sir Gwillym Ff. Williams and the young parson is the Rev. Vivian Thomas

E.G. Williams

CORRIGENDA

Please make the following corrections to Vol. I.

Plate 86C First line should read ''Dai'' Rees, C.B.E. (1913-1983)
Plate 91A Joan Evans was Labour and Co-operative MP for Aberdare from 1974-1979 and for Cynon
  Valley from 1979-1984
Plate 94 Doubt has been cast on the location of this photograph. It is possibly Plasdraw.
Plate 98A Date in line 5 should be 1887 not 1867
Plate 132A Telynog's date of death was 1865 not 1855

Index
of
Plates